Interpreting in Legal Contexts:
Consecutive and Simultaneous Interpretation

by

Debra L. Russell

Linstok Press
4020 Blackburn Lane
Burtonsville, MD 20866
www.signmedia.com

ISBN 0-932130-23-2

How to order:
Single copies may be ordered from **Linstok Press,**
4020 Blackburn Lane, Burtonsville, MD 20866-1667.
For credit card orders, place your order on-line at **www.signmedia.com** or phone **1-800-475-4756.**

Dedication

Dedicated in loving memory of my mother,
Shirley Yvonne Polson (1929-1977)
whose love of books and zest
for learning inspired this journey.

TABLE OF CONTENTS

CHAPTER FOUR:
RESULTS: QUALITATIVE ANALYSIS

CHAPTER FIVE:
DISCUSSION OF RESULTS

ABSTRACT

A comparative analysis was undertaken examining the accuracy of American Sign Language/English (ASL/English) interpreting provided in legal contexts, contrasting simultaneous and consecutive interpreting. Four mock trials were conducted with four ASL/English interpreters. Interpreters worked in teams of two, and participated in three courtroom events: the entering of direct evidence, the cross-examination of the witness and the entering of expert testimony. Interpreters chosen for the study met the criteria of the study and were counter balanced for experience interpreting. Other courtroom participants included judges, lawyers, an expert witness and two Deaf witnesses. The interpretation was videotaped and a sociolinguistic analysis performed on the data to determine its accuracy. All participants participated in post-trial interviews.

Trials with consecutive interpreting were significantly different from the trials using simultaneous interpreting. The consecutive mode demonstrated a greater degree of accuracy than simultaneous. Post-trial interviews revealed themes such as simultaneous interpreting was preferred by lawyers, especially during cross-examination, and judges supported the need for education about how to work effectively with Deaf participants.

It was concluded that the nature of courtroom events require that interpreters know how and when to use simultaneous and consecutive interpreting in order to provide the most accurate interpretation possible to the Court. The implication for interpreters, lawyers, judges and Deaf participants is to examine current interpreting practices and develop and implement guidelines that support accurate interpretation, and full inclusion of Deaf people in the judicial process. The results also have implications for interpreter education programs and professional associations, in terms of identifying whether interpreters are receiving appropriate training in the use of consecutive and simultaneous interpreting, and the specific training necessary for legal environments.

ACKNOWLEDGMENT

I would like to thank a number of people who were instrumental in the completing of this dissertation. First, I would like to express my appreciation to my supervisor, Dr. Aldred Neufeldt. His thoughtful guidance and wisdom were essential ingredients of this work, and served to enhance the experience of completing the writing process. I would also like to convey my gratitude to Dr. Nancy Marlett and Dr. Michael Rodda for their endless support and contributions to this research. I am also grateful for the participation of my dissertation committee members, Dr. Anne Hughson, Dr. Michael Wylie, and Dr. Terry Janzen, for their helpful suggestions, encouragement and challenging questions.

I would like to thank my family and friends for being a constant source of inspiration, love and energy. None of this work would have been possible without the love and support of my husband, Stuart Russell, and our children, Graham and Nicole, who have been patient and encouraging throughout this journey. To my friends, thank you for the many ways in which you supported me throughout all of the stages of this process.

Others who have assisted me in this work are Dr. Jan Humphrey, Karen Malcolm, Janice Jickels, Nigel Howard, Sue Stegenga, Patty Conrad, Kirk Ferguson, Greg Evans, Leanne Walls and Donna Korpiniski. Their insights, editing suggestions, and perspectives taught me so much during this study.

This dissertation was written with financial support from the Social Sciences and Humanities Research Council of Canada, grant No. 752-97-1933, the University of

Calgary, and the Killam Foundation.

My sincere gratitude goes to the people who participated in this study - the interpreters, lawyers and judges, the expert witness, and Deaf witnesses, who were willing to share their time and talent with me. It is my hope that this study contributes to our understanding of how the process of providing meaningful interpretation allows Deaf people true access to legal settings.

LIST OF FIGURES

LIST OF TABLES

CHAPTER 1

INTRODUCTION

During the past thirty years North America has become increasingly sensitive to the social needs and rights of linguistic minorities, resulting in major increases in the use of foreign language interpreting in North American courtrooms (Berk-Seligson, 1990). As well, recognition that native sign languages (NSLs) are legitimate languages, and that Deaf[1] communities are cultural and linguistic minorities, has also resulted in a dramatic increase in the use of sign language interpreters in courtrooms. Despite the increase there have been few empirical studies measuring the accuracy and effectiveness of interpretation services in legal and court settings for either spoken language and sign language interpreters, even though the evaluation of interpretation accuracy is a critical issue for courts and interpreters alike. The focus of this research is the accuracy of sign language interpreting services provided in courtrooms.

Accurate interpretation in legal proceedings requires a level of language proficiency often underestimated by judges, lawyers and court officials involved in the judicial process. A lack of proficient interpretation can give rise to

---

[1] Throughout this dissertation the convention of capitalizing Deaf to distinguish members of a cultural and linguistic group has been used. The word deaf is used to indicate a larger group of people who may or may not be members of the Deaf community, their language or culture not made explicit (for example, deaf students, deaf consumers of interpreting services).

errors which threaten the integrity of the judicial process
(AVLIC, 1994; Berk-Seligson, 1990; Claus, 1997; Colin &
Morris, 1996). For example, Berger (1996) examined the
importance of interpretation accuracy in the context of Deaf
people and allegations of sexual abuse. His findings uncov-
ered that over fifty Deaf people had experienced inaccurate
interpretation during legal investigations and subsequent
trials, which resulted in dropped criminal charges, mistrials
and false acquittals.

There is a significant body of literature on spoken
language interpreting which suggests that consecutive
interpretation[2] allows for a greater degree of accuracy than
simultaneous interpreting[3] (Alexieva, 1991; Bruton, 1985;
Cokely, 1992; Mikkelson, 1995). However, the predominant practice of ASL/English interpreters is to provide
simultaneous interpretation. The present study was designed
to examine interpretation accuracy in courtrooms, specifically when interpreters use consecutive and simultaneous
interpretation strategies. Informed by bilingual interpretation theory from the field of spoken language interpreting,
this study explores and challenges the assumptions that
have prevailed in professional practice and interpreter
education in the field of ASL/English interpretation.
Those assumptions include: simultaneous interpreting is the

---

[2] Consecutive Interpreting is defined as the process of interpreting after
the speaker completes one or more ideas in the source language and
pauses while the interpreter transmits that information (Humphrey
and Alcorn, 1995).

[3] Simultaneous interpreting is defined as the process of interpreting into
the target language at the same time as the source language is being
delivered (Humphrey and Alcorn, 1995).

most accurate form of interpreting; interpreter education programs do not need to teach consecutive interpreting; and providing team interpreting means that the team monitors each other's work, resulting in a high degree of accurate interpretation.

The purpose of this research is to develop a greater understanding of the accuracy of interpreting provided to Deaf participants, lawyers and judges in the context of courtroom events. Exploring and comparing consecutive and simultaneous interpreting used by ASL/English interpreters could inform practice directed at providing accurate service. This research is important for interpreters and interpreter educators. The study will also broaden the understanding of interpretation provided in particular discourse events, and address some of the gaps where there is currently no systematic research about consecutive and simultaneous interpreting with sign language interpreters in legal contexts. Upon completion of this study other researchers could replicate and expand the needed exploration in the area of interpreting in legal contexts.

The research explores the extent to which the current practice of using simultaneous interpretation serves the interests of officials of the court, witnesses and interpreters, and whether this interpreting mode is supported by current interpretation theory or the experience of Deaf people.

This study consists of a comparative analysis of simultaneous interpreting and consecutive interpreting provided by ASL/English interpreters in courtroom interactions. Three distinct courtroom events were studied: expert witness testimony, the entering of direct evidence with a Deaf witness, and cross-examination of the Deaf witness. It also explores consumer satisfaction for the two different types of interpretation. Thus, the present research attempts to assess the accuracy of interpretation provided to Deaf and non-deaf participants in a legal proceeding.

Researcher Position

Komesaroff (1998) suggests researchers who wish to comment on Deaf issues or inquire into the concerns of Deaf people must declare their language skills and experience with Deaf culture. This introduction serves to explain my knowledge of and respect for the language and culture of the Deaf community, my commitment to interpretation that is culturally and linguistically appropriate, and the way in which I view my experiences in the Deaf community from the perspective of an interpreter and interpreter educator.

I am positioned in this study as a non-deaf researcher and interpreter fluent in English and American Sign Language, the language of the Deaf community in Canada. My approach to interpretation has been significantly influenced by my extensive involvement working as an employment counselor, a professional sign language interpreter and an interpreter educator over the past twenty years in the Deaf community. From that blend of experiences comes my deep respect for minority language forms and minority cultures. I began working with Deaf people at a time when research about ASL was just emerging and was being challenged by those who still viewed sign language as an iconic system of rudimentary gestures. It was at this time that I was exposed to Deaf culture and grew to understand the world view of Deaf people, called the Deaf way.

The late 1970's and early 1980's were also years

filled with political and social debate about the best ways to educate Deaf children, what educational supports should be provided to Deaf post-secondary students, and the move to self-determination by Deaf people. As I became more fluent in ASL and became trained as an interpreter, I was struck by the fact that interpreters have a role in providing interpretation that can either include Deaf people as true participants in an interaction or exclude them, by virtue of the accuracy of the interpretation. During the past twenty years I have had extensive experience as a courtroom interpreter, which has led me to question the knowledge base and practices that inform courtroom interpreting. As well, the past ten years of my career have allowed me to participate in intensive training to become an interpreter diagnostician, and to conduct over one hundred diagnostic assessments of the work of interpreters. The analysis of interpreting work has led to greater consciousness about linguistic equivalency and the role interpreters play in providing access to events. When the interpreting work is accurate, access is allowed; when the work is inaccurate or linguistically dysfunctional, access is denied.

As I pursued graduate studies, I completed an oral history project capturing the experiences of Deaf women playing an important role in preserving their language and culture. These pioneer Deaf women were active in publishing Canada's first American Sign Language dictionary. That project deepened my awareness of feminist principles and the nature of language, oppression, and issues of marginalized people finding "voice" as minority cultural members. In the tradition of feminist theory and anthropological discourse (Sen, 1994), I have undertaken to begin this dissertation by discussing the values and influences that have shaped this research study and the perspectives from which I view my research questions, data and analysis.

My professional and academic background has guided my choice of research topic and the structure of the study. Throughout this research I have sought to understand the context in which courtroom interpreters work and how interpreters view their practice. I have also sought to contrast those perspectives with the experiences of judges, lawyers and Deaf participants. How might their experience be impacted by decisions and behaviours adopted by interpreters? What support is required in courtrooms in order for interpretation to be fully accessible to Deaf people? Are there times when consecutive and simultaneous interpretation is appropriate? Inappropriate? What shapes the decisions of interpreters to use a form of interpretation for a particular segment of legal proceedings?

As a non-deaf researcher and an interpreter educator fluent in ASL, I continually negotiate from a position of insider/outsider in the Deaf community. As a fluent user of ASL and an interpreter who still maintains an active interpretation practice, I am defined as an insider by the Deaf community. As a non-deaf person, with no Deaf family members, I am sometimes placed as an outsider by the Deaf community. I also share membership in the same linguistic and professional communities as many of the participants in this study. Finally, I recognize the position of power and privilege attached to the status of researcher.

Overview
Chapter One of this dissertation has provided a context for the study. Chapter Two contains a review of the literature on interpreting, including a description of two of the

dominant theories that have shaped interpreting theory and practice, a review of the ways in which the theories augment our understanding of ASL interpretation, a discussion of legal discourse, and consecutive and simultaneous interpreting strategies. The second chapter concludes with research questions that guided the study described in this dissertation. The results of the study are presented in Chapter Three and Four, followed by a discussion of those results in Chapter Five. Chapter Five ends with a critique of the study and recommendations for future direction in this area. The participants and the methodology of the study are described in the appendix.

Definitions

Throughout this dissertation the convention of capitalizing Deaf to distinguish members of a cultural and linguistic group has been used. The word deaf is used to indicate a larger group of people who may or may not be members of the Deaf community, their language or culture not made explicit, for example deaf students, deaf consumers of interpreting services.

Simultaneous interpreting is defined as the process of interpreting into the target language at the same time the source language is being delivered (Humphrey and Alcorn, 1995).

Consecutive interpreting is defined as the process of interpreting after the speaker completes one or more ideas in the source language and pauses while the interpreter transmits that information (Humphrey and Alcorn, 1995).

Source Language (SL) is defined as the language in which an original message is conveyed, upon which interpretation is based (Humphrey and Alorn, 1995).

Target language (TL) is the language into which a message in interpreted (Humphrey and Alcorn, 1995).

Discourse, for the purposes of this study, refers to language that is uttered by people engaged in social interaction to achieve a goal (Roy, 2000). Discourse analysis can take two forms: structural or functional. Structural analysis involves identifying utterances, analyzing them for grammatical aspects. Functional discourse analysis identifies and analyzes utterances as actions performed by people for specific goals, interpreting social and cultural meaning, and supporting interpretations of the analysis (Schiffrin, 1994).

Utterances refers to the units of language production that are defined by intonation patterns or the completeness of a thought or idea, not as syntactically whole sentences (Roy, 2000). Schiffrin (1994) and Roy (2000) both argue that discourse is best analyzed by examining "utterances", which include structural and functional units of language.

CHAPTER 2

REVIEW OF THE LITERATURE

Overview

The literature review is organized into five sections, each contributing to the theoretical underpinnings. The first section (interpretation theory) presents two dominant theories within interpretation theory and practice which describe the cognitive processes underlying interpretation. A sociolinguistic model of interpretation and a process model of interpretation are examined. A critique of the premises upon which these theories are based, the kind and degrees of research support for the theories, and the level of confidence one might place in them will follow.

The second section defines the ways in which the theories and research help to augment our understanding of ASL interpretation, and the similarities and differences between interpretation where one language is visual (ASL) and the other spoken (English), and interpretation involving two spoken languages.

The third section discusses interpreters and courtroom work. It exposes some of the challenges of legal discourse and the role interpreters play in legal settings.

The fourth section deals with consecutive and simultaneous interpretation strategies. It presents research regarding the characteristics of accurate interpretation and the potential for errors when the cognitive processing time used by interpreters is ineffective in producing an accurate target message.

The last section (present study) presents the specific purposes of the study, the design and the research hypotheses and rationale.

Interpretation Theory

Interpretation processes between languages have been investigated by examining the processes of simultaneous and consecutive interpretation. Interpretation, whether performed simultaneously or consecutively, is a highly complex discourse performance where language perception, comprehension, translation and production operations are carried out virtually in parallel and under severe time pressure (Tommola, 1990). Early research in interpretation conducted by Gerver (1976) and Moser (1978) led to the development of models of interpreting performance based on information processing models. Empirical studies reviewed and described by Goldman-Eisler (1972, 1980), Gerver (1976), Barik (1973,1975), Chernov(1979), and Lambert (1983) focus on the various aspects of input and output, such as the overlap between comprehension and production, the length of ear-voice span, the effect of source text delivery rates or hesitation pauses, and the recall performance of simultaneous interpreters. During the 1980's, Cokely (1985), Colonomos (1983), and Ingram (1985) contributed to a body of literature on simultaneous interpreting with sign language interpreters, describing models of cognitive processing.

This chapter critically examines two cognitive models of interpreting, one based on work with sign language interpreters and one based on work with spoken language interpreters. Cokely (1992) presents a model of sociolinguistic processes based on his study of the work of American Sign Language (ASL)/English interpreters. Seleskovitch (1978) presents a three step model, derived from her work with spoken language interpreters in Europe. Both models are used extensively in schools of interpretation throughout the world, and have served to guide the professionalization of interpreters. A critical review of the premises on which these theories are based follows.

Cognitive Processing Models of Sign Language Interpretation

A body of literature exists specifically addressing sign language interpreting and the major models are reviewed for their critical tenets (Cokely, 1992; Colonomos, 1992; Ingram, 1985; Isham, 1986; Isham and Lane, 1992). The models developed by Cokley (1992), and Ingram (1977) are substantiated by formalized studies of interpretation, while the Seleskovitch (1979) and Colonomos (1988) models are based on the application and interpretation of emerging field research and each developer's experience as an interpreter and interpreter educator. Humphrey and Alcorn (1995) summarized the common components of these models, which apply to both consecutive and simultaneous interpreting:

1. The interpreter takes in the source language utterance;

2. Lexical and semantic units are strung together and held until the interpreter has sufficient units to determine the meaning of what is being said or signed;

3. A string of lexical and semantic units (referred to as a chunk) is analyzed to identify the speaker's intent, the goal(s) s/he wishes to accomplish, explicit and implicit ideas, and a multitude of sociolinguistic features which impact upon the meaning of the source utterance (e.g. gender, power distance between speakers, setting, contextual factors such as the impact or significance of the message on the receiver, etc.);

4. Cultural and linguistic equivalents are sought, observing the cultural norms and cultural overlays of meaning;

5. A search is made of the target language to identify lexical/semantic units and communication behaviours which can be used to produce an utterance in the target language having an equivalent meaning, while maintaining the communication dynamics;

6. The interpretation is expressed in the target language, and;

7. The interpreter monitors internal and external feedback to check for errors or needed corrections.

Colonomos (1988, 1992), building upon information

processing theory, describes the cognitive processes of interpreting as requiring three stages, each with its own cognitive tasks. The first stage is *concentrating*, where the interpreter attends to the source message, quickly and accurately analyzing for meaning; this includes attending (blocking distractions), analyzing and synthesizing to access short-term memory, accessing long-term memory for knowledge and retaining form when appropriate (e.g. proper names). Colonomos refers to *knowledge* as the term for stored (long-term) memory experiences and learning which the interpreter has accumulated in all sensory and intellectual contexts to date. Knowledge may be stored non-linguistically, sometimes in only one language/culture, while other times it may be stored cross-linguistically and cross-culturally. For any given assignment, knowledge refers specifically to knowledge relevant to the message being interpreted.

The second stage, identified as *representing* or *composition*, refers to the interpreter's ability to quickly and accurately construct language forms of the message. This includes retrieval of linguistic and cultural knowledge, ability to access short-term memory, ability to access long-term memory for knowledge, as well as planning the production of the target message.

The third stage is referred to as *planning*, in which the interpreter constructs the target message, attends to discourse frames, identifies elements which cannot be interpreted fully and then delivers the message. This phase of the process is responsible for "supervisory" functions and overseeing numerous cognitive sub-tasks, such as allotting and modifying processing or lag time to allow for analysis/composition; chunking message units into manageable sections; monitoring the sequence of operations; making decisions about obtaining clarification/restatement from the speaker; making decisions about repairing a portion of the target message, and making decisions about seeking support from an external member (team member).

Further, Colonomos (1988, 1992) suggests that the accuracy of interpretation work is affected by the interpreter's preparation, environment and filters. Preparation can include physical dimensions (e.g. sleep, exercise, nourishment); emotional and psychological dimensions (e.g. confidence, stress management); content-related dimensions (meeting with the speaker, researching the topic); and contextual dimensions (e.g. finding out about the participants, environment). Environment refers to any and all conditions that exist at the time of the interpretation. External environmental factors include physical factors (e.g. lighting, temperature, time of day, proximity to speaker/audience/team member, noise). Colonomos uses the term *filter* to refer to the interpreter's own internal environmental factors or psychological "baggage" which may filter in, filter out, or distort any aspect of the message as well as the process factors. No matter how well trained and professional the interpreters, as human beings they have their own biases, beliefs, personality and habits which affect how they perceive people, situations and meaning. The ability to recognize when filters may be affecting the interpretation, and accessing the resources necessary to intervene, may be crucial to the outcome.

Sociolinguistic Model of Interpretation

Cokely (1992) offers a serialized sociolinguistic model of interpretation that has seven major stages:

1. Message Reception
   The subprocess of this stage involves the ability to accurately perceive the source language information, requiring attention as well as visual and auditory recognition skills.

2. Preliminary Processing
   This stage reflects the process of recognizing the auditory or visual input, and the identification of lexical units.

3. Short Term Message Retention
   Stage three involves elaborative operations, where the interpreter decodes the message at various levels: lexical and phrase, sentence and discourse. The message is analyzed and "chunked' into abstract units of meaning and temporarily retained. It is at this stage that the interpreter begins to examine the semantic core of the message, which leads to stage four.

4. Semantic Intent Realization
   Having analyzed and chunked the message, the interpreter comprehends the semantic intent of the speaker/signer. This stage is dependent on the interpreter's source language long-term store.

5. Sociolinguistic factors influencing this stage are described as cross-linguistic and cross-cultural awareness, along with target language long-term store.

6. Syntactic Message Formulation
   After ascribing meaning and determining target language equivalent meaning, the interpreter now formulates the target language message. This stage is influenced by the interpreter's linguistic competence, and their ability to define equivalent linguistic and social markers.

7. Message Production
   The final stage refers to the spoken or signed production of the target language message. It is the form of the final stage that is unique to sign language interpreters, in that there is a modality transfer that does not occur for spoken language interpreters. This stage is influenced by physical and psychological factors and cross-modality issues.

In addition, Cokely contends that stages two through seven are also influenced by further elements such as the interpreter's knowledge of semantics, syntax, contextual information, along with their ability to draw upon associated relations and cultural awareness. Finally, it should be noted that when the interpretation is in simultaneous mode, the interpreter is producing a target language utterance while receiving and analyzing the subsequent source utterance.

Cokely acknowledges that while it is possible to observe and analyze the interpreting behaviour that occurs as a result of the process, it is not possible to observe the cognitive process itself. This means that accurate target language messages and miscues or errors can be identified, but the process that took place that resulted in the interpretation can only be indirectly examined on the basis of observable behaviour. Cokely's model was one of the first to offer definitions upon which to examine and categorize interpretation, ranging from:

- *successful* (meaning the target language adheres to expected language norms and conveys the meaning and intent of the original);
- *deceptive* (meaning the performance has the surface appearance of being successful, but in fact, conveys a meaning or intent different than that of the original);
- *intrusive* (meaning the performance results in errors that deviate from expected language norms; however the consumer can use cloze skills to recover the meaning or intent of the original message); and,
- *dysfunctional* (meaning the performance results in errors that are of such magnitude that consumer recovery of the original message is impossible).

In addition, the model offers ways to categorize the patterns of miscues made by interpreters, ranging from omissions, additions and substitutions, to anomalies.

Premises of the Theory
Cokely (1992) has based his theory of interpretation

on well-established principles in cognitive psychology.

For example, the first stage of the Cokely model is that of attention. Sternberg (1995) describes early neuropsychological studies conducted by cognitive psychologists that defined four main functions of attention (Cherry, 1953, Moray, 1959, Treisman, 1964). Cokely has drawn on two of those features in his model, namely *selective attention,* in which we attend to some stimuli and ignore others, and *divided attention,* in which we allocate our attentional resources to coordinate our performance of more than one task at a time. This first stage is common in most theoretical approaches to understanding interpretation.

Further, Cokely's stages of *preliminary processing* and *short term message retention* (stages two and three) draw upon work from perception studies and theoretical approaches to pattern recognition and text perception and comprehension. Cokely appears to have used constructive-perception theory, which emphasizes the importance of prior knowledge in combination with relatively simple and ambiguous information from the sensory receptors as the foundation for this subtask or stage (Cutting & Kozlowski, 1977). In contrast to this theory, the direct-perception theorists emphasize the completeness of the information in the receptors themselves, suggesting that perception occurs simply and directly, with little need for complex information processing (Palmer, 1975). While both theories have been able to garner empirical support, Sternberg (1995) suggests that humans use a combination of information from the sensory receptors and our past knowledge to make sense of what we perceive.

Stage four of the Cokely model refers to the interpreter comprehending the *semantic intent* of the speaker/signer, which links to premises in reading theory, and specifically studies of text perception and comprehension. Reading theory proposes there are two processes that must be mastered to become a fluent reader: lexical processes and comprehension processes (O'Malley & Chamot, 1996; Sternberg, 1995). Lexical processes are used to identify letters and words, and they also activate relevant information in memory about these words. Comprehension processes are used to make sense of the text as a whole. There are numerous studies describing these processes, some of which are common to most, including semantic encoding, acquiring vocabulary and deriving word meanings from context and comprehension of ideas in texts via propositional representations (Kintsch, 1990; Kintsch and Van Dijk, 1978; Sternberg & Powell, 1983; Sternberg, 1995). These same features are found in Stages Four and Five of Cokely's model, in that the task of the interpreter is to have analyzed and "chunked" the incoming source message and understood the semantic intent of the speaker/signer. Comprehension of the speaker/signer intent is dependent on the level or depth at which that portion of the message has been analyzed. It is further influenced by a number of sociolinguistic factors, including contextual knowledge, knowledge of the syntax and semantics of the source language, the ability to bring previous knowledge to the decoding task, and awareness of cross-linguistic and cross-cultural features.

Cokely describes the processes of decay/forgetting as problems affecting Stages Two through Seven. The lexicon of the Cokely model mirrors the lexicon of memory studies (e.g. level of processing framework, decay theory, rehearsal, short term and long term store, and semantic memory). Sternberg (1995) reviewed several studies on memory and suggests that there is evidence to support decay theory, at least in short-term memory, although it is not definitive. This is also true of rehearsal, which is seen as a key technique for keeping information in storage (Reitman, 1974). In order to transfer information to long-term memory store, an individual must engage in elaborative rehearsal, in which the person structures the items to be remembered in a way that integrates the items more meaningfully into what the person already knows, or meaningfully connects one to another and therefore makes them more memorable (Cooper & Pantle, 1967). It is difficult to study retrieval from long-term memory, due to problems of differentiating retrieval from other memory processes, as well as of differentiating accessibility from availability. Memory studies suggest that the retrieval of information from short-term memory appears to be in the form of serial, exhaustive processing, although some data may be interpreted as allowing for the possibility of parallel processing (Sternberg, 1995).

Discourse involves the units of language larger than individual sentences. Just as grammatical sentences are structured according to systematic syntactical rules, passages of discourse are structured systematically. Cokely states that interpreters need to have a firm grasp of how sentences are sequenced into a discourse structure. Based on knowledge of discourse structure, one can derive meanings of sentence elements that are not apparent by looking at isolated sentences. Research suggests that in order to understand discourse we rely not only on our knowledge of discourse structure, but also on our knowledge of a broad physical, social or cultural context within which the discourse is presented (Dillinger, 1994; Seleskovtich, 1995; Sternberg, 1995). Additionally, Grosz, Pollack, & Sidner (1989) found that the meanings of pronouns, ellipses, definite articles, and other local elements usually depend on the discourse structure within which these elements occur. Cokely suggests that part of the cognitive processing of two languages involves examining cross-cultural and cross-linguistic features of messages, especially at the discourse level. Again, cognitive psychology provides the foundation for the inclusion of these features in Cokely's model.

Cross-cultural and cross-linguistic awareness and knowledge are important underpinnings in Cokely's work, and these aspects appear to be well-grounded in sociolinguistic studies. Studies of bilingualism and biculturalism, pragmatics and how languages are used within a social context, and the nature of shared understanding or scripts provide evidence to suggest that effective communication between bilingual speakers of different languages is dependent on not only a shared lexicon, but on cross-cultural and cross-linguistic awareness (Bialystok and Hakuta, 1994; Cazden, 1988; Cummins, 1976; Seleskovitch, 1994; Tannen, 1990). As well, studies of interpretation accuracy show the grave consequences of not including cross-cultural and cross-linguistic principles that result in literal translations and miscommunication (Cokely, 1983; Claus, 1997; Dillinger, 1994; Taylor, 1993).

Finally, Cokely's model offers ways to describe the error patterns that can occur in interpretation, and ways to categorize the final product. The error pattern analysis structure is based on translation studies (Barik, 1972, Gerver, 1971, Gile, 1985), using common terms such as omissions, additions, substitutions and anomalies. These

terms are also common in literature about reading processes, but Cokely's writing reveals that he was most influenced
by translation theory. It would appear that this error analysis approach reflects best practices within interpretation literature and represents an acceptable methodology in the
analysis of interpretation and translation products (Lambert
& Moser-Mercer, 1997).

Strengths of the Model
        The earliest models of interpretation were founded
on information processing principles, which viewed the
interpreter as a conduit between two languages. As such,
these models did not take into account that the interpreter
mediates between two individuals and communities as well
as mediating between two languages. In this respect,
Cokely's work addresses the study of interpreting processes from a sociolinguistic perspective, enhancing earlier
information processing models by adding sociolinguistic
factors that can occur in a communicative act. Cokely's
model acknowledges the cultural and linguistic differences
between languages, and encourages interpreters to account
for these differences in presenting equivalent messages.
        The model also offers insight into the kinds of errors
that can occur in interpretation, (e.g., omissions, substitutions, additions), and provides a way to describe interpretation from the perspective of error impact on the person
depending on the interpretation, using the terms *successful,
intrusive, deceptive* and *dysfunctional.* For example, *dysfunctional* work refers to an interpretation where the consumer cannot possibly retrieve the original message from
the interpretation; *deceptive* interpretation is work that
sounds or looks like a fluent and plausible message, but it

does not include the message the speaker said/signed (Cokely, 1992).

The model is also helpful from a pedagogical perspective in that it offers a way to teach interpreters to examine miscues and relate the errors to specific cognitive stages hypothesized by Cokely. While there will be miscues for which there is no single cause, such examples do not negate the existence of process stages. Such stages are critical in any examination of interpretation accuracy because they serve as a foundation for interpretation accuracy, offer insight into successful interpretation work, provide a framework for error analysis and suggest the cognitive processes that may account for such errors.

Critique of the Model

A major difficulty with all models of cognitive processing is that interpretation, like other cognitive processes, is minimally a serial process. As Cokely states, "It is likely more accurate to describe the process of interpreting as a serialized parallel process because there are undoubtedly several processes functioning simultaneously in an ordered, dependent relationship to each other".

One oversight of the Cokely model is that there is little emphasis on the importance of decoding speaker/signer goals and discourse frames. Metzger (1995) found that interpreters, like other participants, bring their own frames and schema to interpreted encounters, and when participants do not share the same schema for such encounters it can lead to inaccurate interpretation. Specifically, the Metzger study indicates that interpreted interactions consist of two overlapping dyads, interpreter-Deaf participant and interpreter-hearing participant, with the interpreter as the pivotal overlap engaged in both dyads. In the overlap, the interpreter has the power or ability to clearly influence the discourse within the interaction. Berk-Seligson (1990) in a seminal study of Spanish/English courtroom interpreters, identified ways in which interpreters subtly influenced the perceptions of the speakers for whom they interpreted. Berk-Seligson found that the interpreter is not merely an intermediary in the process, but rather an active participant. Some of the changes influenced by interpreters within a court proceeding included: shifting of registers to more or less formal; adding and/or omitting information; using politeness forms not found in the source message; making statements more or less implicit than they were in the source message, and interpolating cultural information and assumptions. Cokely (1992) has focused on the spoken or signed message alone, and has not accounted for the understanding of speaker/signer goals as an important phase within the decoding and encoding process. Nor has he accounted for the ways that an interpreter can influence the discourse of the interpreted event via frame theory.

A second criticism in the literature stems from the fact that the model is based on the performance of experienced, competent interpreters and as such, it may not account for differences in novice interpreting performances. Dillinger (1994) notes that while simultaneous interpreting has received increasing attention as an object of study (Macintosh, 1985; Henry & Henry, 1987; Gile, 1988), very little of it has been in the form of reliable experimental research. Consequently, little is known about the differences between the work performance of experienced and novice interpreters, and about any possible differences in the way they carry out the task. One school of thought suggests that the skills of interpreters are not characteristic of bilinguals in general; hence the models developed for skilled interpreters do not apply to novice interpreters, and that there are differences in the ways that novice and experienced interpreters perform the task. For example, Dillinger points out some studies have suggested experienced simultaneous interpreters may short circuit the deeper semantic analysis (Gerver, 1976), and that they have been found to add more information and delete less (Barik, 1969), process larger chunks of the input, and give less literal translations (MacDonald & Carpenter, 1981).

A second school of thought suggests that translation ability in general and interpreting skill in particular are natural consequences of bilingualism, and as such, there are few or no differences in the ways that novice and experienced interpreters perform the task, other than quantitative differences in text processing skills (Harris & Sherwood, 1978). This view implies that experience and training have little effect on how the task is carried out. Dillinger (1994) points out that there is no experimental evidence to either support or refute this second position.

Given these two positions, the question of whether there are qualitative differences in semantic and syntactic processing between novice and experienced interpreters may be an important area to examine. The model put forth by Cokely (1992) was based on his study of six interpreters, who were videotaped working at a national linguistics conference. The interpreters serving as research participants were not novice interpreters, but instead had between eight and eighteen years experience interpreting, were all nationally certified, all possessed post-secondary education (bachelor and masters degrees), had between eleven and thirty-one years experience using sign language, and three of the interpreters had Deaf parents and had learned American Sign Language as their first language. Hence, the question remains as to whether the same cognitive model would apply to novice sign language interpreters. To date there are apparently no studies that have examined this area.

A final criticism of cognitive interpreting models such as Cokely's can be found in the writing of Daro (1994) who challenges the idea that a good interpretation necessarily implies the complete understanding and cognitive elaboration of the contents of the incoming message. Daro distinguishes between having a limited knowledge of the basic elements of a huge and complex discipline and claiming to grasp the complete meaning of the speaker's message. As well, Daro believes the hypothesis that a simultaneous interpreter does not often understand the real contents of a message, though he succeeds in translating the 'surface structure" of the input, is representative of current practice. Finally, Daro suggests that it is preferable to have a simultaneous interpreter who is aware of the limitations of her knowledge than one who believes that she understands and runs the risk of misinterpreting or overinterpreting a complex message.

Seleskovitch Model of Interpretation

The second model to be critically examined in this chapter is that put forward by Seleskovitch (1978; 1995). This model is used extensively in schools of interpretation and translation throughout Europe and North America when educating spoken language interpreters. More recently, it has been used in some interpreter education programs working with sign language interpreters (Dr. J. Humphrey, personal communication, March 30, 1998). The model is based on professional practice and learning strategies to enhance interpreting abilities.

Seleskovitch argues that the methodology used in classrooms to teach interpretation should be based on theoretical concepts, and that this fundamental stage in training is the basis for interpreters to acquire the methodology for mastering all interpretation techniques, to learn to dissociate the source and target language and to convey sense. Seleskovitch states that the teaching of consecutive interpretation must serve as the foundation for all other interpreting work, and that if one has not mastered the stages for producing consecutive interpretation, then she can not provide successful simultaneous interpretation. There are three stages to the Seleskovitch interpretation process model:

1. Merging elements of linguistic meaning with extra-linguistic knowledge to obtain sense;
2. Deverbalizing that sense as it emerges; and
3. Spontaneously expressing this sense linguistically.

In the first stage, Seleskovitch guides interpreters to *listen for sense* as the first critical task. She suggests that the interpreter must concentrate wholly on the speaker's intended meaning, picking up on every nuance and subtlety. She offers guidance on where interpreters should direct their attention in the flow of speech, stating that they must learn to disregard the words they hear in order to pay full attention to the message. Listening beyond the words, they will be able to both understand what the words mean and associate their own knowledge to the message. Further, Seleskovitch suggests that interpreters attend to the linguistic meaning or significance of the utterance, and the sense that the utterance takes on in a given context for a given individual. Subtasks or strategies identified within the first stage of the model include: visualizing the message, identifying sequences, listening to figures, associating ideas with terms that have a corresponding term in the target language, identifying the ideas that constitute the message, activating passive memories, reacting mentally and emotionally to the message, and checking fidelity to the sense of the original.

The second stage of the Seleskovitch model is referred to as *deverbalization* which occurs after the interpreter has perceived the sense of a message, and has discarded the linguistic form of the original. The interpreter is now free to express herself naturally in the target language and is able to come up with several possible equivalents, all of which convey the sense of the original equally well. Without deverbalizing, Seleskovitch asserts that interpreters fall back into transcoding (lexical-based translation) and stop interpreting in the true sense.

The last stage is that of *expression of the message into the target language*. Seleskovitch cautions that the temptation to use corresponding terms throughout a text can lead to linguistic borrowing. She emphasizes that expressing oneself in the target language by simply borrowing expressions and structures from the source language results in unintelligibility. An example of such behaviour is speaking "Franglais" versus speaking fluent French. Seleskovitch states that the remedy to this linguistic interference is to deverbalize and completely dissociate the two languages.

Numerous cognitive strategies to aid the interpreter in working through the three stages are outlined by Seleskovitch (1995).

- *Visualizing* is described as using the mind's eye to see an object, or picture the events as they are being described, in order to understand sense.
- *Identifying sequences* is another technique for grasping the sense of the message, in that being aware of the time sequences of a narration and concentrating on each new development as the narrative unfolds can focus one's attention on prioritizing the information according to one specific criterion.
- *Listening to figures* (figures indicating quantities, proper nouns, names and technical terms) for their order of magnitude, in order to maintain the coherence of a text.
- *Associating ideas with terms that have corresponding terms in the target language.* For example, monosemic terms do not need to be interpreted, as they can be transposed from source to target by substituting the corresponding terms that already exists.
- *Identifying the ideas that constitute the message,* where the task for the interpreter is to extract ideas from the spoken message, sort main ideas from secondary or supporting ideas, understand their relative value and properly link them to each other.
- *Activating passive memories,* in which interpreters learn to tap into their own mnemonic ability to identify main ideas and understand the difference between explicit statements and implicit meaning. Seleskovitch states that discourse progresses by

building on what has already been said, with each new utterance presupposing knowledge of what was previously expressed. As the discourse develops the interpreters draw out implicit and explicit meaning by asking themselves probing questions designed to activate their passive memory stores.

• *Reacting mentally and emotionally to the message* by allowing each utterance they take in to provoke some cognitive reaction (idea-associations, knowledge-mobilization) and some emotional reaction (personal stance/response to what is being said).

• The final stage is referred to as *clarity of expression and fidelity to the sense of the original,* in which the interpreter examines the coherence of the text. Clarity of expression comes from understanding the logic of the original, and expressing it clearly in the interpretation. Unlike other models that compare the accuracy of an interpretation with the language used in the original, Seleskovitch judges the interpretation on its consistency with the sense of the original.

Finally, as a result of the above strategies, Seleskovitch asserts that interpreters will eventually see that sense is not the same thing as the sum of the linguistic meanings of individual words and sentences. Rather, sense emerges as these units of linguistic meaning are merged with prior knowledge. This merging process unfolds in the interpreted event. Seleskovitch uses the term "cognitive complements" to reflect the function of the words, and also the knowledge associated with each word. She states that the principle of cognitive complements helps interpreters understand the difference between the sense of a passage of discourse, and the meaning of the linguistic elements used to express it.

Premises of the Theory

Seleskovitch has based her theory on the practical application of learning strategies used when teaching interpreters, rather than on empirical research. Her model is dramatically different from many other interpreting theories. She suggests that traditional contrastive linguistic analysis distorts the concept of translation by taking the final product and inferring the processes that appear to have occurred. Her model, in contrast, sees the expression in the target language derived from a deverbalized sense and not from a manipulation of linguistic elements.

The Seleskovitch model, like the Cokely model, is based on a cognitive information processing view of human thought and action, and theories of second language learning. Information processing studies as well as theories present a framework to explain how information is stored in the memory and how new information is acquired. In its simplest form, the framework suggests that information is stored in two distinct ways, either in short-term memory, the active working memory that holds modest amounts of information for a brief period, or long-term memory, the sustained storage of information, that may be represented as isolated elements or as interconnected networks (O'Malley & Chamot, 1996). In this cognitive psychology paradigm, new information is acquired through a four-stage encoding process involving *selection, acquisition, construction* and *integration* (Weinstein & Mayer, 1986). Through *selection,* learners focus on specific information of interest and transfer that information into working memory. In *acquisition,* learners actively transfer information from working memory into long-term memory for permanent storage. In the third stage, *construction*, learners actively build internal connections between ideas contained in working memory. In the final stage, *integration*, the learner searches for prior knowledge in long-term memory and transfers the knowledge to working memory. The role of learning strategies in this formulation is to make explicit what otherwise may occur without the learner's awareness or may occur inefficiently during early stages of learning. Seleskovitch has highlighted several strategies that focus on the mental processes of shifting information from short-term memory to long-term memory, and she has interwoven the four-stage encoding process into her three-stage model.

Seleskovitch's model closely resembles the work of Bialystok (1978), one of the early theorists who examined second language acquisition and cognitive and strategic processing. Bialystok discussed learning strategies used to exploit available information to improve competence in a second language, suggesting that the strategy used by the learner depends on the type of knowledge needed for a given task. Bialystok discussed three types of knowledge: explicit linguistic knowledge, implicit linguistic knowledge, and general knowledge of the world. Again, Seleskovitch has identified all three types of knowledge in the first stage of her model, and has presented strategies to contribute to the interpreter's ability to comprehend and produce language based on accessing the three types of knowledge.

Further, Seleskovitch has drawn on language comprehension theory (Anderson, 1983; 1985) which proposes that the mental processes necessary for comprehending spoken and written texts are sufficiently similar that comprehension of both can be discussed as a common phenomenon. Anderson separates comprehension into three interrelated processes: perceptual processing, parsing, and utilization. The processes are recursive in that shifts can occur from one process to the next and then back to the previous process. Further, they are consistent and overlap with listening comprehension processes identified in the second language literature (Marmor & Charmot, 1996). Seleskovitch has included perceptual processing, parsing, and utilization in her model, although using slightly different terms, but with the same intent and function.

Anderson (1983, 1985) stated that during *perceptual processing*, attention focuses on the oral or written text, with portions of the text retained in short-term memory. Simultaneously, initial analysis of the language begins, and encoding processes may convey some of the text into meaningful representations. During this process, attention may be directed to aspects of the task or to the context that will be most useful in comprehension. This mirrors the first stage of the Seleskovitch model and some of the initial strategies to focus attention on the sense and context of the message.

In *parsing,* the second listening comprehension process in the Anderson model, (1985) words and phrases are used to construct meaningful mental representations of the text. Anderson suggests that the basic unit of comprehension is a proposition, and once meaning has been determined, it is then reintegrated with the meanings of other propositions to form a more comprehensive understanding of the message. This process is also described in Seleskovitch's model when she emphasizes the strategies of associating ideas with terms that have a corresponding term in the target language and identifying ideas that constitute the message.

The last stage of the Anderson model is *utilization,* where the individual detects or infers meanings and relates that information to existing knowledge. The ways in which existing knowledge is stored, whether as real world knowledge or linguistic knowledge, are then used to aid in interpreting the message. When individuals rely upon meaning-based representations of knowledge to analyze and predict the content of messages they are using top-down processing. Conversely, if they rely upon individual word meanings or grammatical characteristics, they are using bottom-up processing. Seleskovitch implies that interpreters should use top-down processing, while cognitive theory would suggest that effective processing of spoken and written text requires the use of both top-down and bottom-up processing strategies (Howard, 1985, O'Malley & Chamot, 1996).

The process that Seleskovitch refers to as deverbalization may have its roots in second language acquisition theory, the constructs of language proficiency, metalinguistic awareness, the rules of communicative competence, and automatic processing. Metalinguistic awareness is an understanding of the arbitrary uses of language (O'Malley & Chamot, 1996). Tunmer, Pratt & Herriman (1984) assert that metalinguistic awareness is manifested particularly in fluent bilinguals and those individuals typically share advantages not only in verbal skills but in problem-solving tasks as well. O'Mallory & Chamot (1996) suggest that bilingualism has been viewed as "three dimensional insight" into language, a reality rarely experienced by a monolingual. Seleskovitch's description of deverbalization requires the interpreter to possess fluency in both languages, an awareness of arbitrary uses of language, a well-developed sense of communicative competence, and automatic processing. Cummins (1986) suggests that balanced bilinguals have enhanced concept formation and mental flexibility, and it would appear that these attributes are part of the deverbalization process that Seleskovitch finds critical to the interpreting process.

<u>Strengths of the Model</u>

The major strength of the Seleskovitch view of simultaneous and consecutive interpreting is that she has outlined several cognitive strategies (discussed in an earlier section) to focus and enhance the mental processes involved in perceiving the source language, segmenting the message, and then choosing an accurate target language message. From a pedagogical perspective, the strategies put forward by Seleskovitch (1995) have offered educators insight into how to teach the theory of interpreting and they have provided interpreters with the tools needed to produce meaning-based interpretation versus linguistic transcoding.

Seleskovitch's writing has made a significant contribution to the literature through her emphasis on the production of meaning-based interpretation and discourse analysis. She has influenced the interpreting profession to understand interpreting as more than word-for-word transcoding, and her work has served as a foundation for debate, shaping how interpreters think about their work. She was also one of the first educators to define the need to teach and practice consecutive interpretation prior to simultaneous interpretation, believing it to be the foundation for all accurate interpretation work.

Critique of the Model

The major weakness of the Seleskovitch model relates to her view that once comprehension has been achieved, the structure of the source language has no further role in simultaneous interpretation. Little experimental work has been performed that tests her claim about dever- balization (Giles, 1990), and most of the literature is either theoretical or descriptive in nature (Gran & Dodds, 1989). However there is some experimental work that points to the importance of comprehension as a necessary stage to accu- rate interpretation, as seen in studies of lag time, ear-voice spans, and units of meaning necessary to form propositions (Cokely, 1993; Gerver, 1876; Isham, 1996). Isham (1996) suggests that there is no evidence to verify that propositions are actively processed, only that they are available before the target language message is produced. Isham and Lane (1993) conducted an experiment with professional inter- preters, examining whether interpreters process incoming sentences in the same way as listeners do, and whether they would have the same pattern of recall. The premise was that if interpretation requires more (or less) focus on the source language structure, this should be reflected by better (or poorer) recall, thus testing Seleskovitch's claim that interpreters completely deverbalize a message prior to tar- get language production. The results showed that, contrary to Seleskovitch's assertion (1975), information about the form of the source language sentence was available to the interpreters. In partial support of Seleskovitch, Isham and Lane (1993) reported that the interpreter appeared to lose the memory trace for sentence form sooner than listeners did, indicating a greater tendency to process information clause by clause, rather than sentence by sentence.

In a more recent study, Isham (1996) found that interpreters did not deverbalize any more than listeners did, yet they produced fluent, comprehensible French renditions of the source language input. Thus, Isham suggests that we should understand deverbalization as one possible stage of interpretation, rather than a required one, at least when interpreting between English/French. Isham, however, points out that a strict word-for-word transcoding is not possible or desired in interpretation, due to the differences found between any two natural languages. Hence one could expect evidence of deverbalization and meaning-based interpretation work when the difference in grammars between language pairs becomes greater and greater (e.g., English-Mandarin Chinese).

Lastly, while deverbalization may be the goal within accurate and intelligible interpretation, it is difficult to put into practice in the classroom in that very few students come into training programs with a strong command of two non-interfering, self-contained linguistic systems (Seleskovitch, 1995). This is due in part to the way foreign languages are taught, which still places a great emphasis on the substitution of terms, and the fact that many students have not learned their second language in a rich linguistic environment. These factors make it rare for the student interpreter to begin interpreting from this understanding, rather than resorting to transcoding.

While Seleskovitch has not rigorously tested her theory, her writing has informed interpreting practice and makes intuitive sense to those familiar with interpreting processes.

Relevance to ASL/English Interpretation

The value of the two different cognitive models to ASL/English interpretation is that both models offer guidance into understanding the nature of processing information and restructuring it into a second language. Both Cokely (1992) and Seleskovitch (1995) advocate for interpretation that acknowledges the differences in linguistic and cultural meanings between two languages, and a representation of meaning-based work.

Both models have drawn on literature from cognitive theory, specifically information processing theory, second language acquisition, and bilingualism. What is problematic in both models is the lack of empirical studies to support them and therefore the evidence is preliminary at best. Cokely provides a model based on theory and one small sample of professional interpreters. Seleskovitch appears to have based her model entirely on theoretical principles and teaching practices. The inferences made from the theoretical literature seem helpful and plausible in describing the basic processes of perceiving, restructuring, and composing messages between two languages, but there is very little evidence that these are in fact the strategies or processes that interpreters use in order to provide accurate interpretation.

Seleskovitch (1995), uses the word "strategy" loosely, but as Isham (1996) points out, its correct meaning in cognitive terms denotes conscious control. To date, no one has tested whether interpreters actually have conscious control over the techniques they use. In this light, Isham questions whether we should be labeling the approaches used in interpretation as "strategies" or "processes".

From an educator's point of view, the two models described in this paper have been useful in teaching interpreters, in that they have allowed a highly complex mental process to be broken down into steps that can be handled by the interpreter. Further, Seleskovitch's emphasis on consecutive interpretation as the foundation upon which to acquire solid interpreting abilities has made a valuable contribution in the teaching of interpreters, and has influenced professional practice. It would appear that Seleskovitch's model assists in teaching interpreters and also gives interpreters the tools they need in order to provide accurate interpretation.

Given the complexity of the mental processes involved in interpretation, there are also descriptive studies that have examined the differences between consecutive and simultaneous interpretation, and that provide support for the Cokely (1992) and Seleskovitch (1995) models. Consistently, the evidence suggests that consecutive interpreting results in much greater accuracy in the transmission of the message (Alexieva, 1991; Bruton, 1985; Cokely, 1992; Mikkelson, 1995). Alexieva (1991) found that the practice of simultaneous interpreting has shown that not all types of texts can be interpreted under the difficult conditions characterizing the material (e.g. simultaneity of the speaker's and interpreter's performance, speed of the delivery of the source language, lack of knowledge about the context, and a single rendition of the source utterance). Barnwell (1989) concurs with this view, stating that simultaneous interpretation offers very little time to reflect on the linguistic choices needed for a precise rendering. Bruton (1985) agrees with Seleskovitch, arguing that in order for interpretation to be successful it must include the reformulating and retransmitting of concepts into the target language. It must also produce the same impact or impression on its audience as that created by the speaker on an audience which understands the message directly. Further, there is agreement within the literature that consecutive interpreting, working from memory and notes, makes it easier to break down the interpreting process and examine the skills required to cope with the process successfully (Alexieva, 1991; Barnwell, 1989; Bruton, 1985; Mikkelson, 1995). Lastly, Bruton (1985) and Lambert (1989) emphasize that a progression of exercises aimed at teaching interpreters to grasp, analyze, remember, and only subsequently, reproduce the message of the speaker, makes it possible for student interpreters to proceed to acceptable simultaneous interpretation where required or desired. All of these studies point to a framework in which consecutive interpretation can strengthen the accuracy of interpretation, but the evidence is based on a very small number of studies.

Cokely (1992) examined simultaneous interpretation among ASL/English interpreters, and his findings demonstrated a critical link between the length of time between speaker utterances and the target language production, and the rate of interpreting errors. He reported that one of the primary causes of misinterpretation appeared to be the lack of sufficient source language input, which is determined by the interpreter's processing time. The shorter the lag time, the greater the probability of inappropriate target language syntactic constructions and lexical choices in the target language, and the greater the tendency for the interpreter to adhere to source language syntax, which results in word-for-word based transcoding. Given this reality, consecutive interpretation is being reconsidered as a viable option by ASL/English interpreters working in mental health and legal settings.

Despite the significant body of literature from spoken language interpreting which suggests that consecutive interpretation allows for a greater degree of accuracy, the predominant practice of ASL/English interpreters is to provide simultaneous interpretation. As well, despite literature that suggests consecutive interpretation strategies must be learned prior to learning how to provide simultaneous interpretation, only two out of the six interpreter training programs in Canada devote course work to consecutive interpretation, and use it not only as a foundation skill upon which to build simultaneous interpretation skills, but as a valuable work-place approach to interpretation. The question arising from such practice is this: Are consumers, both Deaf and non-deaf, receiving accurate and effective interpretation when the majority of interpreting service is being provided in simultaneous format?

Similarities and Differences: Spoken and Signed Languages

There are many similarities between spoken language interpretation and sign language interpretation, resulting in common national and international conferences of interpreters regardless of whether the working language is a spoken or a signed language. As well, during the past ten years, mainstream professional journals and interpretation texts have regularly published studies of research on sign language interpretation. There is widespread agreement between academics and interpreting professionals that the shared interests are greater than the differences.

The cognitive models of interpretation, regardless of philosophical differences, share a common approach to the comprehension of the source message, restructuring between two languages, and then the production of the target language. Additionally, both spoken language and sign language interpreter education programs are teaching cognitive models of interpretation, and their professional accreditation exams require demonstration of using process models in the application of meaning-based interpretation (Roberts, 1996).

The striking difference between spoken language interpreters and sign language interpreters is that sign language interpreters not only work between two languages, but two modalities. This modality shift is noted in the Cokely (1992) model, but there appear to be very few studies that have examined this difference (Corina & Vaid, 1996). It is this modality difference, involving an auditory-temporal language and a visual-spatial language, that has also contributed to the predominant use of simultaneous interpretation. The use of simultaneous interpretation can occur more readily for sign language interpreters as there is no need for technology or pausing, in that the interpreter can sign while someone is speaking and speak while someone is signing, without the languages interfering with each other.

Interpreters and Courtroom Work

The importance of accurate interpretation in legal settings appears to have been well documented (AVLIC,

1994; Claus,1997; Cokely,1993; Berk-Seligson,1990; Colin & Morris,1996). In order for Deaf people to have an equitable legal experience in the courtroom, ASL/English interpreters must possess the requisite skills and knowledge in order to perform in this complex setting. The following sections outline the relevant literature on interpreters and courtroom work, and simultaneous and consecutive interpretation.

During the past thirty years, with America's growing sensitivity to the social needs and rights of linguistic minorities, there has been a tremendous increase in the use of foreign language interpreting in North American courtrooms (Berk-Seligson, 1990). American statistics indicate a threefold increase in the use of interpreters in courtrooms during the period from 1970 (Berk-Seligson, 1990). Interpretation accuracy has been critical since the 1978 enactment of the United States Federal Court Interpreters Act (Public Law 95-539), which ensured non-English speaking and hearing impaired defendants [sic], litigants, and witnesses access to court-appointed interpreters.

In Canada the use of both spoken language interpreters and sign language interpreters is relatively commonplace. The Canadian Charter of Rights and Freedoms, Section 15, has stimulated a greater use of interpreters for Deaf people in provincial and federal court matters. An example of the use of interpreters stems from the period of 1995 to 1997 when the province of British Columbia recorded at least 21 weeks of court time where teams of ASL/English interpreters were provided for Deaf participants, compared to only four weeks of court time which required interpreters during 1993-1995 (personal communication, Still Interpreting, Feb. 16, 1997). Further, in

October, 1997, the Supreme Court of Canada ruled that health care settings must provide sign language interpreters for Deaf clients, finding that sign language interpreters are necessary for effective communication in the delivery of medical services, and the failure to provide them in British Columbia constituted a denial of s. 15(1) of the Canadian Charter (Eldridge v. British Columbia, October 09, 1997). Legal advocates within the Deaf community suggest that this ruling will have a significant influence on the increased use of professional interpreters in all aspects of life, including legal settings.

The use of competent court-appointed interpreters is critical to the conduct of fair legal proceedings. The Ministry of the Attorney General in British Columbia has begun to study ways in which to improve the delivery and quality of interpreting services offered to Deaf participants (personal communication, Pat Elsom-Lewis, Dec. 01, 1997). Similarly, the state of New Jersey commissioned a study of court interpreting services, finding that non-English speakers were not being served adequately through interpreting services. As a result, the Attorney General in that state is currently re-writing policies, offering training and certification for court interpreters, and seeking input from non-English minorities about how best to address the problems of courtroom interpretation (personal communication, R. Roberts, January 04, 1998).

When to use interpreters and how to ensure competency and availability, however, can be problematic (Morrow, 1994). Legal interactions are inherently complex, and when participants do not share a common language, the need for interpreters is clear. At the same time, the act of interpreting accurately is enormously difficult in any setting (Berk-Seligson, 1990; Cokely, 1992; Morrow, 1994; Schein, Mallory & Greaves, 1991, Taylor, 1993). Interpreting is not the straightforward process that it is often assumed to be, in which a virtually invisible person acts as a conduit. Several difficulties arise, such as the difficulty in finding lexical equivalents for complex legal terminology, the extra time which must be added into the proceedings to accommodate the interpretation process, and the lack of education among court personnel about the importance of hiring competent interpreters. As Morrow (1994) suggests, the court will often resolve the problem of lengthy court proceedings by limiting the use of interpreters and expediting the process. Linguistic problems are often seen, by the court, as resolvable by having interpreters engage in preparation and use dictionaries and lexical lists. However these procedures have not proven effective in dealing with the many sociolinguistic complications inherent in the interpreting process.

Legal Language

The emphasis on terminological equivalencies can distract attention from several larger and more diffuse aspects of courtroom communications: the challenges inherent in the varieties of language used by legal personnel themselves, the other shades of meaning inherent in messages which cause analysis challenges and errors in the interpretation, and the various cultural differences that complicate the interpretation process (Berk-Seligson, 1990; Morrow, 1994).

The courtroom is one of the most complex communicative settings that a lay person is likely to encounter. In the courtroom, an unusual alternation of linguistic registers ranging from formal to informal are employed within a single proceeding. To participate effectively in legal proceedings, the interpreter must be able to ideally comprehend and interpret successfully among these challenges. Lawyers and judges routinely gauge the impact of their speech, in terms of intelligibility and/or persuasiveness, on various listeners.

At the most informal levels, for example, lawyers work to create solidarity with jurors by frequently using colloquial English; they also have recourse to a standard English register that is somewhat more formal than their own everyday speech. As Morrow (1994) identifies, depending on their own verbal repertoires, and on their judgment of the seriousness of the situation, jurors, witnesses, defendants and other lay participants may formalize their speech to a register seen as more impressive or credible. They may also use subcultural varieties of English. A judge may signal a less solemn moment with humour, intended to put the nervous participants at ease and simultaneously reinforce his/her own prerogative to set the communicative tone of the court from moment to moment.

Morrow (1994) also found that legally educated speakers alternate all of these "ordinary" English modes with the most formal register of legal English, which is characterized by jargon, complicated syntax, and features otherwise found only in written discourse. Formal legal language, in fact, frequently consists of written texts rendered orally (such as routine jury instructions, which judges have memorized verbatim). Formal legal English differs from other (written and spoken) forms of English lexically, syntactically, and at the level of the discourse. Interpreters must understand all of these in order to work effectively.

Challenges of Legal Language

There are a number of features of legal language which make it challenging to understand, and difficult to interpret accurately. O'Barr (1982) and Danet (1980) identified that language used in legal processes is characterized by:

1. technical terms;
2. common terms with uncommon meanings ("assignment");
3. words with Latin, French, or Old English origins ("voir dire");
4. a high percentage of polysyllabic words ("collateral");
5. unusual prepositional phrases ("in the event of default");
6. paired, redundant words ("will and testament; freely and voluntarily");
7. formality;
8. vagueness; and
9. over precision.

Similarly, Berk-Seligson (1990) and Morrow (1994) state that legal English has the following linguistic challenges:

1. the use of noun phrases where verbs would be more commonly used ("make assignment" instead of "assign");
2. frequent passive constructions ("remedies may be

provided by the law");

3. unusual conditionals   ("in the event of default");
4. frequent repetitions of the same noun instead of an initial use of a noun followed by pronoun references ("the party of the first" never becomes "he");
5. "whiz deletion" which is an absence of forms like "who is" or "which are", resulting in phrases like all the rights and remedies available to the secured party";
6. complex lengthy sentences;
7. odd determiners ("such" and "said");
8. numerous negations;
9. impersonality: preference for third person over the first person (references to "the party", "the borrower" as opposed to "I" and "you");
10. parallel structures linked with "and" or "or"; and
11. lists of sentences strung together less cohesively than in standard written or spoken English and overly compact phrases which include a great deal of information in one sentence with little or no rephrasing.

These aspects make formal legal English both dense, and challenging, to understand.

Mallory (1994) and Berk-Seligson (1990) stress that speakers utilize all of these features (formal legal English, standard English, colloquial English, various subcultural varieties of English) in a subtle interplay driven by necessity and strategy. As with all communications, language in the courtroom is a complex social interaction. Additionally, the interaction is constrained by procedural rules that are largely unknown to the lay persons involved. For example, the law necessitates that specific forms, which cannot be easily paraphrased, be used for the record in certain contexts.

As Morrow (1994) states, this results in effectively excluding lay persons from such conversations between judge and lawyers, who share a common idiom but also a common legal "culture", that makes their exchanges more efficient by allowing much of the message to be left implicit.

The adversarial nature of the legal system also dictates that lawyers use language strategically to both control testimony and convince a judge and jury to a particular interpretation of the facts. Individual styles, class, age, ethnicity, and gender add further layers of communication complexity. Educated speakers of English find this a challenging situation, and it becomes an even further challenge for speakers of languages that are not English and who have limited experience in or understanding of the legal system.

Because formal legal English is so different from ordinary spoken English, the difficulties of interpreting it receive the most attention. However, what is probably most difficult about the interpreter's task is the need to manage the constant interplay of all of these linguistic varieties and registers in a single event (Morrow, 1994; Witter-Merithew, 1995). The presence of non-English speakers and speakers of English as a second language further complicates this situation. If cultural and linguistic differences exist even among English speakers, the use of languages other than English increases the potential of interpretation problems. These potentials are greatest when the languages in question (such as American Sign Language and many immigrant languages) are linguistically unrelated to English. In such cases, the semantic domains of words and expressions and the sociolinguistic conventions employed by speakers are rarely congruent between languages (Cokely, 1993; Morrow, 1994).

Interpreters, no matter how competent, bilingual, and bicultural they may be, must constantly weigh choices in search of the best ways to convey shades of meaning and speaker intent (Morrow, 1994; Smith, 1996; Witter-Merithew, 1995). They must also deal with the cultural differences that are embedded in the linguistic structures. For example, the narrative structures, the depth of detail in a description, and the social fabric of a culture that is different than the language of the majority create incredible challenges for an interpreter when attempting to convey equivalent sense so that all parties can participate equally.

The evaluation process is the foundation of legal proceedings; everyone present decides moment to moment the degree to which other speakers are accurately, intelligently, and credibly representing their actions, observations, understandings and experience. The evidence on which participants base their evaluations is thus overwhelmingly sociolinguistic - they judge what people say and how well they say it (Colin & Morris, 1996; Isham, 1988; Morrow, 1994). When courtrooms employ the use of interpreters, the interpreters are one more element affecting the mutual evaluation of speakers.

Susan Berk-Seligson (1990), in a seminal study of Spanish/English courtroom interpreters, identified the variety of ways in which interpreters subtly influenced the perceptions of others about the speakers for whom they interpreted. Berk-Seligson states that the interpreter is not merely an intermediary in the process, but rather an active participant. Some of the changes influenced by interpreters within a court proceeding included: shifting of registers to more or less formal; adding and/or omitting information; politeness forms; making statements more or less implicit than they were in the source language, and interpolating cultural information and assumptions (Berk-Seligson, 1990). Berk-Seligson also documented instances where interpreters interrupted lawyers and witnesses, or prompted witnesses' responses. Morrow (1994) found that all these behaviors affect the evaluation of a speaker's credibility, knowledge and status, in addition to more obvious types of miscommunication that interpreters attempt to repair by stopping to explain cross-cultural/linguistic differences, or by asking for clarification from the speaker.

Consecutive and Simultaneous Interpretation

Cokely (1992) suggests that the need for interpreter services has its earliest documentation in legendary accounts (e.g. Tower of Babel), as well as the historical accounts (e.g. the conquests of Alexander the Great) of antiquity. Clearly, for thousands of years, interpreters have been used to facilitate minority linguistic interactions with members of the majority linguistic community. This is most apparent when one examines the linguistic and communicative interaction between Deaf and hearing communities. Until relatively recently, all interpretation used consecutive interpreting methods, but after World War II, at the Nuremberg trials in Germany, the simultaneous method of interpreting received much attention (Adams, 1997).

Technological advances made it possible to use simultaneous interpreting in these trials. Further, a time savings was realized because the interpreters translated the message at the same time as they heard it uttered. Since the Nuremberg trails, simultaneous interpreting has become widespread practice.

Consecutive interpretation, in which the interpreter waits until a complete thought has been spoken and then begins interpreting is the primary form used in medical situations (Mikkelson, 1995). A very high standard of accuracy prevails in consecutive interpretation. It allows for the conveyance of the content of the source language message, as well as critical information conveyed in the structural elements of that message that are not contained in the words: pauses, tone of voice, stress, etc. Many interpreters regard consecutive as the most difficult mode of interpreting because it is so challenging to retain all of these aspects of the source language message, particularly when a question or answer is very lengthy or is not entirely coherent (Mikkelson, 1995).

On the surface the use of simultaneous interpretation can occur more easily for sign language interpreters because of the two different language modalities, a visual-spatial language and an auditory-temporal language. This requires no technology or equipment, and no pauses, in that the interpreter can sign while someone is speaking and speak while someone is signing without the modality of each language overlapping. This may account for the ready acceptance of simultaneous interpreting practices within the field of sign language interpreting.

While consecutive and simultaneous interpretation methods each have merits, research in the interpreting field has consistently shown that consecutive interpreting results in much greater accuracy in the transmission of the message (Alexieva, 1991; Bruton, 1985; Cokely, 1992; Mikkelson, 1995). Given this context, consecutive interpretation is being reconsidered by sign language interpreters as a better way of working in court and legal settings. Depending on the Deaf and hearing consumers and the nature of the proceedings, court interpreters may use consecutive or simultaneous methods, or a combination of both methods of interpretation within a single proceeding. Decisions about whether to use consecutive interpreting are sometimes made when the information is complicated or technical, when the Deaf person has a non-standard or unusual language variation or when the language depends heavily on metaphors or illustrations.

Alexieva (1991) found that the practice of simultaneous interpreting has shown that not all types of texts can be interpreted, under the difficult conditions characterizing the material (e.g. simultaneity of the speaker's and interpreter's performance, great speed of the delivery of the source language, lack of knowledge by the interpreter about the context, and a single rendition of the source utterance). Barnwell (1989) concurs with this view, indicating that simultaneous interpretation offers very little time to reflect on the linguistic choices needed for a precise rendering of the information into the target language. Bruton (1985) states that in order for interpretation to be accurate and successful, it must not only include the reformulating and retransmitting into the target language, but is must also produce the same impact or impression on its audience as the impact or impression the speaker wishes to create on an audience which understands him directly. Similar to

Alexieva and Barnwell, Bruton suggests that the most accurate form of interpretation is consecutive interpreting,
because it allows for the interpreters to draw upon their
skills of word fluency, ideational fluency (the ability to call
up ideas where the quantity and quality of idea is emphasized), expressional fluency (the ability to think rapidly for
appropriate wording of ideas) and associational fluency (the
ability to produce words from a restricted area of meaning).
There is agreement among authors that consecutive interpreting, whether working from memory or notes, makes it
easier to break down the interpreting process and examine
the skills required - not just the skills of the various fluen-
cies but also the considerable intellectual qualities required
to cope with the process successfully (Alexevia, 1991;
Barnwell, 1989; Bruton,1985; Mikkelson, 1995). Further,
Bruton (1985) and Lambert (1989) emphasize that it is
through a progression of exercises aimed at teaching the
interpreter to grasp, analyze, remember, and only subsequently, reproduce the message of the speaker, that interpreters eventually proceed to acceptable simultaneous
interpretation where required or desired.

Summary of the Review of the Literature

The studies reported here provide a theoretical foundation for understanding interpretation, and the cognitive
processes relied upon when the interpreter is performing
simultaneous or consecutive interpretation. Given that the
interpreting process is, in part, serialized (that is, certain
cognitive activities are prerequisites for and prior to other

cognitive activities), difficulties encountered in the initial stages of the process will affect later stages of the process (Cokely, 1992). Despite these challenges, the models put forward by Cokely (1992), Colonomos (1992) and Seleskovitch (1994) are used as pedagogical tools to encourage all interpreters to examine miscues and to relate them to each of the cognitive stages hypothesized by the authors. As Cokely identifies, there will be miscues for which there is no one cause, but such examples do not negate the existence of the process stages. The process stages are critical in examining the accuracy of interpretation because they serve as the foundation for interpretation accuracy, offer insight into successful interpretation work, provide a framework for error analysis, and suggest the cognitive processes that may account for such errors.

The literature regarding courtroom interpreting and the challenges present in such work point to the potential for grave errors. However, there is a lack of research about the accuracy of interpretation in legal contexts when provided in a consecutive approach versus a simultaneous approach. It is clear that than any examination of accuracy of interpretation must rely on miscue identification and the links between the error pattern and the cognitive processes involved in producing an equivalent message.

The literature suggests that there are times when consecutive interpretation renders a more accurate message in legal contexts, but there are no studies that specifically examine consecutive interpretation when applied by ASL/English interpreters in the courtroom. Hence the need for the current study.

Research Questions and Legitimacy
of this Inquiry

The research questions for this study center on the issue of the accuracy of interpretation provided to Deaf and non-deaf participants in courtrooms, which has an impact on Deaf people's legitimate and complete access to court proceedings. The study explored how interpreters provide interpretation within a legal context, and their beliefs and attitudes towards the work. The study was also an opportunity to examine some of the products of the interpreters' cognitive processing, in the form of their notes used in preparing for the consecutive interpretation. Associated with these questions were issues such as the education that interpreters have had prior to working in legal settings, their experiences working in interpreting teams, the nature of error management in highly stressful situations, and the role of preparation when interpreting in trial processes. Further questions arose surrounding the experience and the beliefs held by Deaf people about the interpreting process and accessing court proceedings via ASL/English interpreters. Additionally, questions from the perspective of non-deaf agents of the court arose, such as: What is the experience of the court using interpreters? Do lawyers and judges have preferences about how the interpreting is conducted or is their primary concern accuracy? What knowledge do lawyers and judges have about interpreters and the issues surrounding bilingual interpretation of legal discourse? These questions and issues offered direction to the research, but they were not restrictive.

The legitimacy of a study into the accuracy of simultaneous and consecutive interpretation has been established in the review of the literature in this chapter. Such a study has not been carried out in North America and this study contributes to the knowledge base about interpretation pedagogy and practice. With the increasing need for competent interpreters in legal contexts, there is a need for research-based information to guide policy and practice. In this study, I sought to understand the nature of legal discourse frames and when simultaneous and consecutive interpretation could most effectively provide an accurate message.

Rationale for the Current Study

Although current theory and research appear to support the need for accurate courtroom interpretation, the absence of studies focused on sign language interpreters leaves many important questions unanswered. Specifically, five key reasons supporting the evaluation of the accuracy of interpreting services include the following:

1. There is widespread agreement among experts in the field of interpretation that the principle of accuracy of courtroom interpretation is extremely important to the integrity of the legal system and to ensuring non-English speakers have equitable access to justice. At the present time there is no agreement about what constitutes a qualified interpreter and how to evaluate the effectiveness of interpreting services (AVLIC, 1994; Berger, 1994; Claus, 1997; Morrow, 1994; Colin & Morris, 1996). Additionally, there appear to be few studies which can inform such policy decisions.

2. There is also considerable documentation about the complex linguistic and cultural challenges that face interpreters attempting to provide accurate bilingual and bicultural interpretation (Berk-Seligson, 1990; Cokely, 1992: Colin and Morris, 1996; Morrow, 1994). These challenges stem from the features of legal language that make it challenging to understand, and difficult to interpret accurately, the register and formality frequently used in courtrooms, and the adversarial nature of the courtroom proceedings (Danet, 1980; O'Barr, 1982). Further it is clear from the literature that in order for some of those linguistic and cultural complexities to be addressed in a trial process, interpreters must engage in effective preparation with those involved in the interpreted event (AVLIC, 1994; Berk-Seligson, 1990; Witter-Merithew, 1995). However, systematic measurement of interpreting processes, both simultaneous and consecutive, should be undertaken directly rather than through inference based on studies of simultaneous interpreting strategies.

3. From studies of spoken language interpreting and of cognitive processing, there are strong arguments in favour of consecutive interpreting producing more accurate work (Alexieva, 1991; Barnwell, 1989; Bruton, 1985; Cokely, 1992; Lambert, 1989; Mikkelson, 1995). Despite such evidence, the prevalent practice is to provide simultaneous sign language interpretation in courtrooms. Little research exists to guide the field of sign language interpretation as to which process - consecutive or

simultaneous - leads to the most accurate interpretation. Consequently, there is a need for research on how sign language interpreters are functioning in the courtroom, and how the accuracy of the interpretation might be improved by examining the differences between consecutive and simultaneous interpretation.

Research questions requiring attention include: What are the characteristics of accurate interpretation? What role does preparation play in trial processes? What insight into the initial cognitive processes of comprehension of the source message and reconstruction in the target language can be gleaned from an examination of the notes taken during interpretation?

4. To date there appear to be no studies that have examined the use of American Sign Language/English interpretation in legal settings. At this time, only one British study (Brown et al, Durham University, in press) has evaluated the unique variables in a legal context that affect interpretation between two languages differing in their modalities. The study explored interpretation where one language is an auditory/oral language like English and the other language is a visual/spatial language like British Sign Language. Hence, the question arises, is there a difference in the accuracy of courtroom interpretation when the provision of interpreting service is simultaneous versus consecutive when there is a difference in modalities?

5. Finally, there is little research that includes the experience of those relying on interpretation, namely Deaf people and agents of the court. What are the experiences of Deaf people and agents of the court when accessing court proceedings through the use of ASL/English interpreters?

Research Objectives

The existing literature in conjunction with research on case studies, sign language interpretation and courtroom interpretation guides the following research objectives.

Objective 1

To investigate and compare the accuracy of ASL/English interpretation when interpreters are using simultaneous interpreting processes versus consecutive interpreting processes.

Objective 2

To investigate the experiences of those involved in courtroom interactions by conducting personal interviews with interpreters, deaf and non-deaf witnesses, lawyers and judges.

Objective 3

To investigate the preparation strategies of interpreters when working together as a team, when preparing lawyers about the task of working with interpreters, and when preparing with Deaf witnesses.

Objective 4

To explore two aspects of the cognitive processes of interpreting (source language comprehension and target language composition) by examining the notes taken by interpreters and used as interpreting tools while interpreting a trial.

CHAPTER 3

RESULTS: MOCK TRIAL ANALYSIS

The primary purpose of this study was to examine the differences in courtroom interpretation when the service was provided in simultaneous or consecutive mode. The first section of this chapter presents the analysis of data collected across the four trial events, and then presents further data from the individual trials. The trials using simultaneous interpreting are presented first, followed by the trials using consecutive interpreting.

Discourse Events In Trials

During courtroom proceedings a number of distinct discourse events can take place; for example, the calling to order by the clerk of the court, the introduction of Crown and defense attorneys, the calling of the first witness, expert testimony, direct evidence, cross-examination and summation of trial positions. For the purposes of this study, three distinct discourse events within each trial were analyzed: expert testimony on ASL linguistics, Deaf culture, and interpretation was presented in spoken English and interpreted into ASL; direct evidence from Deaf witnesses was given in ASL and interpreted into spoken English, and the questions put to the witness were interpreted from spoken English to ASL; and cross-examination of the same Deaf witness required both ASL and spoken English interpretation. Each discourse event had goals reflecting the role of the participant speaking or signing in that event.

During expert witness testimony there were several goals to be achieved, with the purposes varying per participant. For example the Crown prosecutor wanted to achieve the goal of having the witness accepted by the Court, and to enter credible testimony that would serve as a foundation for the case. The judge interjected comments with the goal of expediting the qualification process, and later asked specific questions designed to solicit expert opinion. The defense lawyer posed questions with the goal of challenging some aspects of prior testimony and exploring new areas of testimony.

While direct evidence was being entered the Crown prosecutor used language to purposefully present the Crown's case in the best light possible, and to present the facts per the natural sequence of events. By contrast, the linguistic goals of the defense lawyer during cross-examination were to expose inconsistencies within the testimony and suggest an alternative narrative or explanation for the events in question.

The interpreters faced the challenge of interpreting the questions and answers placed to witnesses, taking into account the structural elements and the functional or goal elements. The elements taken into account by the interpreters included appropriate lexical and grammatical features, social or contextual meanings, and possibilities to elicit a response (Roy, 2000). When analyzing the data, determinations of interpreting success or errors also included these same structural and functional elements (Dillinger, 1999).

Results of the Quantitative Analysis

Transcripts of the four trials were analyzed for interpreting accuracy, interpreting errors by interpreting mode and discourse event, and errors per discourse events and the target language used by the interpreters. Further, tests of significance were conducted. Interpreter generated utterances were also identified and reported.

Accuracy Rates across Trials

Table 3.1 summarizes the overall accuracy for each of the trials. The two trials using consecutive interpreting demonstrated a higher degree of accuracy as compared to the two trials where simultaneous interpreting was used.

TABLE 3.1
Overall Accuracy of Interpretation by Type and Trial

Trial No.	Interpretation Mode	Accuracy (%)
Trial 1	Simultaneous	87
Trial 2	Consecutive	98
Trial 3	Consecutive	95
Trial 4	Simultaneous	83

In Trial One, 87% accuracy was achieved. Conversely, this represents 13% of the trial's total utterances that involved interpreting errors. By contrast, Trial Two had 2%

errors over the duration of the trial. Trial Three, which was also performed using consecutive interpreting, demonstrated a 95% accuracy rate with a 5% interpreting error rate. Lastly, Trial Four had a 83% accurate rate, and a 17% interpreting error rate.

Error Rates across Discourse Events

Table 3.2 indicates the number of interpreting errors per discourse event as a proportion of the total number of utterances.

TABLE 3.2
Interpretation Errors by a Ratio of Total
Utterances by Trial and Discourse Event

Discourse Event

Trial No.	Expert Witness	Direct Evidence	Cross-Examination
Trial 1	21/213*	39/189	15/188
Trial 2	5/292	4/154	1/157
Trial 3	27/353	6/193	3/188
Trial 4	32/202	45/185	17/175

* Note: To be read as 21 errors out of 213 total utterances

As can be noted in Table 3.2, the number of interpreting errors across discourse events is greater for expert witness and direct evidence discourse events. For all four trials, there are fewer errors exhibited during cross-examination.

The data were pooled and tested for significance using Chi Square Tests. Results of the error analysis per the three discourse frames were used as the dependent variables, with the type of interpreting (Consecutive and Simultaneous) as the independent variable. The results of the Chi Square Test for the Expert Witness Discourse Event are shown in Table 3.3, and clearly there are significant differences.

TABLE 3.3
Type of Interpretation with Accuracy of
Interpretation for Expert Witness Discourse Event

Evaluation of Interpretation	Consecutive	Simultaneous	Total (N)
Correct	613 95.04%	362 87.23%	975
Incorrect	32 4.96%	53 12.77%	85
Total N Total %	645 100.00%	415 100.00%	N=1060

Chi square = 20.188, df=1, p<0.001: Phi = 0.14, p<0.001

Table 4.3 shows there is a statistically significant association (Chi Square = 20.88, df = 1, p<0.001: Phi =0.14, p<0.001) between the error rate and the type of interpretation in the expert witness discourse form. For the consecutive interpreting mode, 95.04% of utterances were correct, as compared to 87.23% of the utterances using simultaneous interpreting.

The results of the Chi Square Test or the Direct Evidence Discourse Event are shown in Table 3.4.

TABLE 3.4
Type of Interpretation with Accuracy of
Interpretation for Direct Evidence Discourse Event

Evaluation of Interpretation	Consecutive	Simultaneous	Total (N)
Correct	237 95.95%	290 77.54%	527
Incorrect	10 4.05%	84 22.46%	94
Total N Total %	247 100.00%	374 100.00%	N=621
Chi square = 39.25, df=1, p<0.001: Phi = 0.25, p<0.001			

Table 3.4 shows there is a statistically significant association (Chi Square = 39.25, df = 1, p<0.001: Phi=0.25, p<0.001) between the error rate and the type of interpretation for the direct evidence discourse form. For the consecutive interpreting mode, 95.95% of utterances were correct,

as compared to 77.54% of the utterances using simultaneous interpreting.

The results of the Chi Square Test for the Cross-Examination Discourse Event are shown in Table 3.5.

TABLE 3.5
Type of Interpretation with Accuracy of
Interpretation for Cross-Examination Event

Evaluation of Interpretation	Consecutive	Simultaneous	Total (N)
Correct	241 98.37%	331 77.54%	572
Incorrect	4 1.63%	32 8.82%	36
Total N Total %	245 100.00%	363 100.00%	N=608
Chi square = 13.55, df=1, p<0.001: Phi=0.15, p<0.001			

Table 3.5 shows there is a statistically significant association (Chi Square = 13.55, df = 1, p<0.001: Phi=0.15, p<0.001) in the error rate and the type of interpretation for the cross-examination discourse event. For the consecutive interpreting mode, 98.37% of utterances were correct, as compared to 77.54% of the utterances using simultaneous

interprcting.

These Tests of Significance suggest that the consecutive mode of interpretation is superior to the simultaneous
form, when used for all three discourse samples.

Errors by Target Language

The results of the total number of interpreting errors
per target language across all four trials are summarized in
Table 3.6. The target language for the interpreters working
with the expert witness was ASL, while direct evidence and
cross-examination required the interpreters to demonstrate
both spoken English and ASL as the target languages.

TABLE 3.6
Total Number of Interpreting Errors per Target
Language and by Trial

Discourse Event	Target Language	Trial Number / Interpreting Mode*			
		1-S*	2-C*	3-C	4-S
Expert Witness	ASL	21	5	27	32
Direct Evidence	ENG	22	3	3	27
Direct Evidence	ASL	17	1	3	18
Cross-Exam	ENG	7	0	1	7
Cross-Exam	ASL	8	1	2	9

* Note: "S" means simultaneous interpreting and "C" means
consecutive interpreting

Table 3.6 shows the total number of interpreting errors per target language. When working into ASL, the interpreters made a greater number of errors compared to when they were working from ASL to spoken English. Of interest is Trial Two where there were no errors made during cross-examination when working from ASL to English.

As well, there were consistently more errors produced when the target language was ASL. For many interpreters, ASL is a language they develop as their second language, after acquiring spoken English. Three out of four interpreters in this study identified ASL as their second language, with the exception of one individual who has Deaf parents and therefore ASL was a first or native language. The errors made interpreting into spoken English were also influenced by this feature, in that the majority of errors were comprehension related. When interpreting from ASL to English, the interpreters could produce fluent English, but the message was inaccurate, resulting in a deceptive message.

There is an interesting difference between Trial Two and Trial Three. Both trials were conducted using consecutive interpreting; however in Trial Three some unusual events took place. In each of the trials, the interpreters had agreed to split the expert witness testimony with each interpreter working approximately 20 minutes per segment. In Trial Three this did not occur. The interpreters did not switch, which resulted in the same interpreter working the entire 60 minute segment. Despite using consecutive interpreting strategies, the interpreter began to make numerous linguistic errors after 30 minutes, which is consistent with what is known about mental and physical fatigue experienced by interpreters. The interpreter used

notetaking strategies to improve the accuracy of the work
(see p. 106); however it did not result in the kind of accuracy seen in Trial Two.

Across all four trials the cross-examination discourse events show far fewer errors than the other discourse
events. This was an expected result in that the evidence had
been entered via direct testimony, and cross-examination is
an opportunity to refute that same evidence. The interpreters had previously interpreted the witness's evidence, so
were therefore prepared for the cross-examination of the
witness. There was nothing substantially new that arose
during cross-examination, and hence the accuracy rate was
higher across all four trials when contrasted to the other two
discourse events.

Error Patterns across all Trials

An examination of the transcripts reveals that common patterns of errors emerged from all trials, including the
following:

- Omission of content;
- Shift of tense (mixing of present tense for past
  tense);
- Shift of register (more casual in ASL than indicated
  in the source message of English);
- Deceptive ASL to English messages (message was
  produced in fluent English, but presented inaccurate
  content);
- Dysfunctional grammar when representing English
  to ASL messages;

- Source language intrusions which resulted in form-based or transcoding work; and
- Interpreter created utterances which were not interpreted for all participants.

Interpreter Generated Utterances

The interpreters sometimes generated utterances in addition to those by the lawyers, judge, and witnesses. This occurred at times when the interpreters directly addressed the Deaf witness without indicating to the judge or lawyers that they were seeking clarification. There were other utterances also generated by the interpreters, which occurred when the interpreter clarified or corrected an earlier interpretation. On occasion, the interpreter clarified an answer in spoken English while the other interpreter signed the message in ASL. Conversely, there were also times when the clarification from the interpreter was in spoken English only, excluding the Deaf witness from the information.

Table 3.7 represents the number of interpreter generated utterances created in each trial, and whether they were made accessible in both languages, were signed only, or spoken only.

TABLE 3.7
Interpreter Generated Utterances per Trial and
Language used when Generating the Utterance

Trial No.	Total Utterances	Language Used		
		Signed/ Spoken	Signed Only	Spoken Only
Trial 1	7	4	2	1
Trial 2	6	2	2	2
Trial 3	14	3	8	3
Trial 4	6	3	1	2

Table 3.7 shows more frequent interpreter generated utterances in Trial Three. Also of note in Trial Three are the number of utterances that were signed only, meaning that the judges and lawyers had no access to that information. Trials One and Four show there were more occasions when the interpreters represented the utterances in both languages, making the utterances accessible to all courtroom parties.

As Berk-Seligson (1990) demonstrated in her study of courtroom interpretation, interpreters are not always simply interpreting. They interrupt proceedings to seek clarification, to have statements repeated and to make requests. The interpreter generated utterances in this study follow similar patterns. The interpreters sought clarification from lawyers when questions were vague, and also sought clarification from Deaf witnesses about the specific features of an answer. The interpreters sought permission from the judge in order to seek clarification, but in this case, not all utterances generated by the interpreter were interpreted and made accessible to all court participants.

Summary

The quantitative results demonstrated the success rate was greater for trials using consecutive interpreting as compared to trials using simultaneous interpreting. There were more interpreting errors found in the trials using simultaneous interpreting, and the majority of interpreting errors were created during expert witness testimony and the entering of direct evidence. The results also show a greater number of errors when the target language was ASL. Lastly, in each of the trials, interpreters created utterances in addition to those of the lawyers, judges and witnesses. There were times when these utterances were made accessible in ASL and spoken English, and other occasions when the utterances were not accessible to all courtroom participants, as they were either created in only ASL or only spoken English.

Results by Modality of Interpretation

The following section describes the data in greater depth per each trial. The two trials that used simultaneous interpreting (Trials One and Four) will be presented first, followed by the two trials in which consecutive interpreting (Trials Two and Three) was used. Each trial will be analyzed by examining the preparation strategies, notetaking use, success rates, error patterns and unique features.

Simultaneous Interpreting Trial Data

Trial One: Interpreter Preparation Strategies

This trial was conducted in a simultaneous interpreting modality whereby the interpreters used simultaneous interpretation for all segments.

Two interpreters were assigned to the trial. Prior to the trial, they held a preparation conversation between themselves about how to function as a team. They chose to split the expert testimony into two sections, with each interpreter providing interpretation for 17 minutes. In this discourse event, there was only one target language, which was ASL. Each interpreter, when not actively interpreting, was seated facing the other interpreter, monitoring the accuracy of the work. Occasionally, the interpreters would supply each other with information needed to provide an accurate message.

The interpreters made different decisions about how to split the interpreting when dealing with the Deaf witness testimony which required both ASL and spoken English as target languages. One interpreter provided the ASL to English interpretation and the other interpreter provided the English to ASL interpretation. Both interpreters monitored the accuracy of the work being produced by their interpreting partner, and offered corrective information when necessary in order to present an accurate message. Despite this precaution, several errors were made across the three discourse events that were not caught and corrected by the team.

Trial One: Notetaking

During Trial One, the interpreting team placed

notetaking materials within their reach, but during the preparation conversation they did not address how they could be used. During this trial, neither interpreter used the notetaking materials.

Trial One: Success Rate per Total Utterances
     The trial took one hour and five minutes to complete. There were a total of 213 utterances during the expert witness testimony, 189 utterances during the direct evidence portion, and 188 utterances during the cross-examination of the Deaf witnesses. This trial had an overall success rate of 87%.

Trial One: Examples of Successful Interpretation
     The following five examples will illuminate success across each of three discourse events: expert witness, direct evidence and cross-examination. In each example, the discourse event is identified. The speaker's utterance is identified, followed by the interpreter's rendition of the original message. For the interpreted rendition, the writing convention of using capital letters is used.

1. Expert Witness Testimony

     Lawyer: So the process is the same whether it is
                 ASL or English, right?

     Interpreter: INTERPRETING PROCESS - ASL
                   INTERPRET SPOKEN ENGLISH OR
                   HEAR ENGLISH INTERPRET ASL
                   MENTAL PROCESS SAME RIGHT?

The interpretation had an equivalent message and incorporated all of the features of discourse goal, affect, intent, and grammar successfully. The interpreter chose a grammatical structure known as "compare and contrast" in order to present the mental processes of interpreting. The "compare and contrast" structure allowed for presentation of the information to be established in ASL space, and then consistently referenced as it was in the spoken English message. The example was spatially referenced, using separate linguistic spaces in order to map the concepts of producing ASL to English and English to ASL.

2. Expert Witness Testimony

Witness: ASL is a visual spatial language that has its own grammar, syntax and semantic categories. The language is typically referred to as a topic language in that the topic is followed by the comment, if I may give you an example of that...

Interpreter: WH? VISUAL - SPATIAL LANGUAGE - OWN GRAMMAR, RULES, SYNTAX, SENTENCE STRUCTURE AND MEANING SIGN MEANING. ASL (PAUSE) PAH TOPIC - COMMENT LANGUAGE -SET TOPIC FIRST, FOLLOW COMMENT, OFFER EXAMPLE CAN I?

In both example one and example two, the topic of discussion was one that is familiar to ASL/English

interpreters and the interpreter did not have
to process the information at a deeper level
in order to discover the meaning. Based on
their prior knowledge, they could effectively use their prediction and language closure
skills to create an equivalent message.

3. Expert Witness Testimony

Witness: ASL is an interactive language much like
Japanese and the examples I gave earlier.
The head nodding does not indicate agreement but rather means HAI HAI HAI - it
is offering information that tells the signer
that I am with you, I am following you, but
it doesn't imply agreement.

Interpreter: ASL LANGUAGE MEAN WH? TWO
PEOPLE CONNECT BACK FORTH
COMMUNICATE ... SAME IDEA
JAPANESE REMEMBER BEFORE
SAID JAPANESE TWO SPEAKERS
TALK ONE SPEAKER NOD
UNDERSTAND SAY....(pause 5 sec) ..
HAI HAI HAI NOT MEAN YES
AGREE MEAN I UNDERSTAND.
DEAF SAME IDEA ASL SIGNER
TALK-TO-ANOTHER ASL SIGNER
ASL SIGNER MUST HEAD NOD
WHY? SHOW I UNDERSTAND KEEP
GOING MEAN AGREE NOT MEAN
THAT.

In this example the interpreter successfully used a compare and contrast strategy, and the use of space to compare ASL and Japanese. The interpreter referred back in space to the earlier topic of Japanese language patterns and drew upon visual strategies to compare the "head nodding" to the vocal utterances made by a Japanese speaker. The interpreter seemed to pause and hesitate before indicating the HAI HAI HAI portion of the message, but presented it with sufficient context for the receiver of the message to understand the emphasis was on the interactive nature of language, and not on the actual words said between speakers of Japanese.

4. Direct Evidence

Witness: SO, I ASKED BOYFRIEND TO BRING COOLER ...PEACH COOLER BUT HE BROUGHT HOME KIWI - I HATE KIWI COOLERS SO DIDN'T DRINK MANY OF THEM.

Interpreter: So, I asked my boyfriend to bring me some coolers back from town, and I specifically asked for peach coolers, but he brought back kiwi flavoured coolers. I hate the taste of kiwi coolers so I didn't have many of them.

In example four, the interpreter drew on their knowledge of cultural and semantic accuracy in order to produce a message that made sense, observed English grammatical properties and offered sufficient context for the consumer to understand the message.

5. Cross Examination

Lawyer: Isn't is true that you consented to have sex with my client and then when your boyfriend found out you changed your story and accused Jason of this assault?

Interpreter: TRUE, YES - NO - WHICH? YOU - JASON - AGREE HAVE SEX LATER BOYFRIEND YOURS HEARD MAD YOU INVENT STORY BLAME JASON FORCE SEX TRUE?

This example demonstrated an equivalent message and the speaker's intention was realized through the signs chosen and the affectual components put to the message. The question angered the witness and prompted an emotional response.

Trial One: Error Rate per Total Utterances

Table 3.8 indicates the number of interpreting errors per discourse event as a proportion of the total number of utterances for Trial One.

TABLE 3.8
Interpretation Errors by a Ratio of Total
Utterances and Discourse Event: Trial One

Discourse Event	Errors per Utterances	Percentage of Error (%)
Expert Witness	21/213*	10
Direct Evidence	39/189	21
Cross-Examination	15/188	8
Total Trial Utterances	75/580	13

* Note: To be read as 21 errors out of 213 total utterances

The majority of errors in this trial occurred during direct evidence, with 22 errors in the ASL to English work and 17 errors in the English to ASL work. During cross-examination there were 8 errors in the English to ASL work and 7 errors in the ASL to English work.

When providing interpretation it is impossible to create a "perfect" interpretation, but the question to be asked in this context is "What error rate is acceptable in a courtroom setting?"

Trial One: Examples of Unsuccessful Interpretation
    There was a 13% interpretation error rate for this trial, and the following examples will illuminate unsuccessful interpretation in utterances across each of three discourse events: expert witness, direct evidence and cross-examination.

1. Expert Witness Testimony

Witness: So we might use the analogy that an idea is "clothed"...

Interpreter: LANGUAGE LIKE PRETEND PERSON CLOTHING CHOOSE

In this example, the interpreter did not identify the topic of an "idea", so the comment which follows did not make grammatical sense in ASL. The message was not equivalent based on the omission of topic and the substitution of PRETEND PERSON instead of using a conventional ASL strategy for describing analogies.

2. Expert Witness Testimony

Witness: ASL is a high context language, and by that I mean...

Interpreter: IMPORTANT UP TO NOW INFORMATION

The topic and comment of this utterance was completely omitted in the interpretation, and a processing time check revealed that the interpreter was two seconds behind the speaker. Such a processing time does not allow for the interpreter to uncover the meaning, or restructure the message into ASL.

3. Direct Evidence

Witness: NO   I DID NOT CONSENT TO HAVE SEX

Interpreter: No, no - It was all his idea.

This example showed an error of content which left a different impression than intended by the Deaf witness. The witness was specific in the answer, identifying the proposition of not agreeing to have sex and the implicit message of BIG HEAD ENTER AGREE NOT may have been more accurately conveyed as "What an arrogant guy - coming into my bed like that - NO - I did not agree to have sex with him." The omission of specific content was critical in this answer.

4. Direct Evidence

Lawyer: So your boyfriend knows you pretty well, right?

Interpreter: BOYFRIEND TOGETHER LONG TIME
SEEN DRUNK BEFORE YOU KNOW?

Witness: No.

In this example the interpreter misinterpreted the question, and linked the target language construction to a previous utterance about the length of time the witness had been with her boyfriend, and whether they had been drunk together on previous occasions. This inappropriate cohesion to past information resulted in an answer of "NO" when the predicted answer was "yes". The witness looked evasive in their answer, based on the interpretation. The witness was presented with a different question in the target language than in the source language.

5. Cross-Examination

Witness: HIM (ACCUSED) SIGN... COMMUN-
CATE WELL? HA - HE CAN NOT
SIGN HIS WAY OUT OF PAPER BAG...
LIKE SAY HI! GREAT! AOKAY! THAT
SIGN? ASL?...NOT FLUENT AT ALL -
GESTURE ONLY - NOT SIGN LAN-
GUAGE - TYPICAL HEARING
PERSON

Interpreter: Jason can't sign very well. He knows
some ...ges - some signs, well just social

graces, like gestures, that is all.

This interpretation was not accurate in that the tone and intent of the message was lost. The shift to formal register also did not reflect the original register in ASL, and the loss of specific examples detracted from the meaning of the original message. There were false starts which affected the accuracy of the message as well.

Trial One: Error Patterns

During Trial One the interpreters checked with each other on eight occasions during the direct evidence. Despite checking with each other, the errors were not corrected, leaving inaccuracies in the interpretation. These comprehension checks were a subject of concern for lawyers and judges and will be discussed in the interview section of Chapter Five.

An error pattern which emerged in all three discourse events was the choice of a register which did not reflect the speakers. For example, the lawyers and judge remained formal with each other, and referred to the witness by their professional title. The sentence structure and lexicon of their questions indicated a consultative and formal register, yet there were examples of the interpreters choosing a register in ASL that is typically reserved for close acquaintances in a casual setting.

Another type of error emerged in the form of source language intrusions from spoken English to ASL. An example would be when the interpreters presented interpretation that had the surface grammar of English, which is also referred to as form-based work. The meaning was not clear and these kind of errors forced the Deaf person to perform the "interpretation or translation" in their own minds. Deaf people have a particular sign for this phenomena and in the post-trial interviews, the Deaf witness stated that at times they were doing the "figuring out" or "interpreting in their head". There were several utterances when the interpreter was working from spoken English into ASL where source language intrusions were present, and in these instances the Deaf witness asked for clarification of the question. These requests for clarification seemed to serve as a cue to interpreters, as the next few utterances were more deeply processed in order to present meaning-based interpretation.

There also were times when interpreters appeared to struggle for English choices to describe ASL concepts that had more of a cultural context in the source language. An example of this relates to when the interpreters were trying to convey in spoken English the concept that the hearing person accused of the crime could only use gestures and was not a fluent signer. The Deaf witness had several choices to describe the person's inability to use sign language, and the interpreter was not able to produce an equivalent message; the spoken English was awkward and marred by false starts.

Trial Four: Interpreter Preparation Strategies

This trial was conducted by interpreters using simultaneous interpretation. As with Trial One, there was a team of two interpreters assigned to the trial, who held a preparation conversation which resulted in similar working processes as the previous trials. These decisions included splitting the expert witness testimony in 18-20 minute blocks, and later dividing the interpreting process when dealing with the Deaf witness. Positions and cueing were handled in the manner of Trial One.

During the preparation conversation, the interpreters negotiated how to handle errors. Several errors that arose during the trial were handled in the manner discussed, and some errors were overlooked by both interpreters.

Trial Four: Notetaking

In the preparation conversation, both of the interpreters acknowledged that they were not in the regular practice of taking notes during courtroom assignments. They agreed to have the materials available, but they were not used in the trial.

Trial Four: Success Rate per Total Utterances

The three distinct events of the trial took one hour and twenty-five minutes to complete. There were a total of 202 utterances during the expert witness testimony, 185 utterances during the direct evidence portion, and a total of 175 utterances during the cross-examination of the Deaf witnesses. The trial had an overall success rate of 83%, which was the lowest of all four trials.

Trial Four: Examples of successful interpretation.

The examples of successful interpretation demonstrate the same patterns as in Trials One, Two and Three. However, three practices which occurred in this trial and contributed to successful interpretation are described further.

1. Use of both consecutive and simultaneous interpreting.
   During the trial one of the interpreters switched into

using consecutive interpreting for a segment of utterances initiated by the judge. Prior to the entering of direct evidence, the judge posed a number of questions to confirm the Deaf witness's understanding of the meaning of taking an oath. The interpreter working from spoken English into ASL used consecutive interpreting to hear the complete utterance of the judge, in order to structure the message using a contrastive approach for the taking of an oath versus affirming. The judge and interpreter appeared to negotiate the consecutive interpretation through eye gaze and the interpreter's behaviour: The interpreter stopped interpreting in the simultaneous mode, appeared to be listening for meaning, then the interpreter looked at the judge and nodded to him, which signaled him to stop, followed by the interpreter delivering the interpretation.

When the interpreter used consecutive interpreting for this section of the trial, the message was thoroughly processed and there were fewer instances of relying on discourse markers to link ideas. Discourse markers or cohesion ties are the ties and connections which exist in text. A number of discourse markers are used in English and ASL (e.g., however, but, understand, mean). Instead, the ideas were consistently presented as they were in the source message, as distinct thoughts.

After the oath process was completed the interpreter returned to using simultaneous interpreting for the questions that were factual in nature - for example, where the witness attended school, her age, and the predictable questions leading up to the witness describing what brought her to court that day. When the witness began to describe the nature of events that surrounded the court case, the interpreter chose to use a very long processing time (22 sec.), while demonstrating a number of ASL attending behaviours designed to tell the witness to continue (nodding at the Deaf witness), and then interpreted the answer into spoken English. While this work was not totally consecutive, it was accurately conveyed by utilizing the increased processing time. The application of the ASL attending behaviours was a source of concern for the judge and lawyers, however, who had no frame of reference for why the interpreters appeared to be "encouraging" the witness.

2. Decision making processes and interpreter generated utterances.

During this fourth trial, the lawyer asked the interpreter to repeat an answer as the interpreter's voice was too soft to be heard. The interpreter addressed the judge, seeking direction: "The whole answer?". The judge responded: "No, just the ending". While this interaction was taking place, the second interpreter, performing the English to ASL work interpreted the conversation between lawyer/judge/interpreter. Further, as the ASL to English interpreter repeated the last phrase, the second interpreter signed what the interpreter was saying. All of the decisions reflected practices which had the effect of keeping the Deaf witness informed of what was happening in the courtroom, while respecting the needs of the lawyer and judge for repetition of an answer.

3. Overlapping discourse.

During cross-examination, the lawyer posed the following question:

> "Have you ever misbehaved in class before - ?"
> The judge then interjected, by saying:
> "I don't know if that is an appropriate question..."

The interpreter had completed some of the interpretation, noted the judge's interjection, then continued to offer the remainder of the question before including lawyer/judge interaction. The interpreter turned their body slightly away from the witness and there was no eye gaze towards the witness, so it was clear that the witness was not involved in this interaction as yet. The interaction was completed simultaneously, and accurately reflected the overlapping discourse.

Trial Four: Error Rate per Total Utterances

Table 3.9 illustrates the number of interpreting errors for Trial Four per discourse event as a proportion of the total number of utterances.

TABLE 3.9
Interpretation Errors by a Ratio of Total
Utterances and Discourse Event: Trial Four

Discourse Event	Errors per Utterances	Percentage of Error (%)
Expert Witness	32/202*	15.8
Direct Evidence	45/185	24.3
Cross-Examination	17/175	9.7
Total Trial Utterances	94/562	17.0

* Note: To be read as 32 errors out of 202 total utterances

In Trial Four an 83% accuracy rate was achieved by using simultaneous interpreting strategies. The majority of errors in this trial occurred during direct evidence, with 27 errors in the ASL to English work and 18 errors in the English to ASL work. During cross-examination, there were 9 errors in the English to ASL work and 8 errors in the ASL to English work. Such a pattern of errors is particularly problematic, given that the lawyers, judges, and Deaf witnesses have no way to monitor if the work is accurate. They operate on faith that the interpretation is accurate when in fact it is not.

Trial Four: Examples of Unsuccessful Interpretation.

The following examples present a summary of some of the errors which emerged in this trial. The presentation of these error examples is different from Trial One, in that it categorizes the error type prior to the example being presented.

1. Inconsistent Interpretation of the Oaths

Each of the interpreters took a standard courtroom oath that asked them to "well and truly interpret" during the court proceeding. In this segment, Interpreter A took the oath in spoken English, while Interpreter B interpreted the oath for the Deaf witness's benefit. The interpreters then switched positions and repeated the process. The interpreters took identical oaths in spoken English, but the interpretations looked very different. After the interpreters were sworn, the Deaf witness was sworn. Interpreter A interpreted the oath to the Deaf witness, and used a different ASL interpretation of the meaning of the oath. The oath is known as a segment of "frozen text", in that the words are always identical, and never change. By contrast, the interpretation during that five minute period demonstrated three different versions of the oath.

In ASL the oath reflected the following differences:

Interpreter A:
Spoken English: "...promise to interpret to the best of your skill and ability....so help you God."

ASL: "...GOD HELP YOU?"

Interpreter B:
Spoken English: "...promise to interpret to the best of
                    your skill and ability....so help you
                    God."

ASL: "...GOD WATCH YOU?"

Interpreter A:
Spoken English: "...truth and nothing but the truth....so
                    help you God?."

ASL: "...WHOLE TRUTH, NO LIES, ZERO
                    ADD STORIES, PROMISE? GOD
                    JUDGE"

When interviewing the Deaf witness after the conclusion of trial, the witness questioned why the interpreters
had not chosen one standard interpretation and been consistent in its use. There are standard accepted versions of other
forms of frozen text, for example, the Lord's Prayer, and in
most contexts that include frozen texts, teams of interpreters
generally agree upon the form and use it throughout the
assignment.

When checking the transcript of the preparation
conversations held between the interpreters prior to interpreting the trials, none of the teams in any of the trials discussed the oath prior to the trial.

2. Overuse of Discourse Markers to Link Ideas

Throughout the simultaneous interpreting work,
both interpreters appeared to overuse discourse markers, for

example, the ASL discourse markers glossed as "understand", "mean" and "plus". In one five minute segment, a frequency count revealed the use of 20 discourse markers. In fact, Topic/Comment structure would have been more natural and allowed for consistent topic reference as opposed to linking every idea to the previous idea.

3. Source Language Intrusions

As with the first trial performed using simultaneous interpreting, there were more source language syntax intrusions present in this trial than in the consecutive trials. An example of such follows:

Expert Witness Testimony

Lawyer: Let me make sure, it says you have testified some 60 times....Does it have a date...

Interpreter: ME MAKE SURE...EXPERT WITNESS 60 TIMES.....D-A-T-E, have?

In example two, the "make sure" was a source language intrusion and was followed by the absence of a verb relating to actual testifying. The topic of discussion was implied, that of the curriculum vitae, but the reference to the topic was not in the interpretation.

4. Register Shifts

As with the previous trials, one of the problematic patterns that arose in this trial was that of register shifts made by the interpreters. The spoken English was consultative, but in several sections the register in ASL was representative of more casual ASL, as in the kind of language used between two people who know each other well. In this court context, the expert witness and the agents of the court were not familiar or known to each other and hence used a consultative or formal register.

Expert Witness Testimony

>   Witness: I was assigned to an interdisciplinary team
>   which was pulled together to respond to
>   allegations of sexual abuse at Jericho School
>   for the Deaf. We were to examine the quali-
>   fications necessary within the interpreting
>   teams working at all phases of the investiga-
>   tion and subsequent trials.

In this example, the answer was offered in a consultative register but when compared to the work that was presented in ASL, the register appeared much more casual than the original message. The interpretation was suitable per grammatical construction but choice of register made it look like a much more informal answer.

5. Source Language Pausing and Phrasing Patterns

When contrasted with Trial One, which was also conducted using simultaneous interpreting, there was a consistent pattern between the two trials, in that the ASL interpretation followed the pausing and phrasing patterns of English. The interpreters had little time between question and answer to structure the interpretation so that it reflected more ASL-like behaviors. When the interpreters did take the time, a processing time of approximately 14 seconds behind the source language was demonstrated. When the interpretation does not observe the language norms of ASL per pausing and phrasing strategies it is very visually "busy" and if there are not frequent breaks, it can be very fatiguing for the Deaf consumer. One Deaf witness likened it to a "snowstorm" of information, but noted that because it was expert witness testimony, and not their own testimony, she was less worried about ensuring she fully followed it. While the nature of expert testimony can be fast-paced and complicated, there are ways to manage the information and still present it in ASL grammar which were not utilized here.

6. Omissions

During this trial, between minutes 41:30 - 49:30 there were 13 omissions which skewed the accuracy of the message. The expert witness was answering questions about the accuracy of interpretation in courtrooms and the interpretation did not reflect an equivalent message. For example:

Lawyer: ...should we focus on the demeanor of the deaf person or attend to the sign language?

Interpreter: Focus on ASL or listen interpretation.

In this example the interpreter has deleted the feature of "demeanor", which has changed the intent of the message.

Consecutive Interpreting Trial Data

What follows is a summary of the data from Trials
Two and Three which were both conducted using consecutive interpreting.

Trial Two: Interpreter Preparation Strategies
In this trial the two interpreters used consecutive
interpretation. As in Trials One and Four, during the preparation conversations the interpreters agreed to work as a
team in the same manner. This means they agreed to split
the expert testimony in two sections, with each interpreter
providing interpretation for 20 minute segments. The interpreters positioned themselves as the interpreters did in Trial
One, so that when the second interpreter was not actively
interpreting, they were seated facing their interpreting partner, monitoring the accuracy of the work.

The interpreters in Trial Two also made the same
decisions as interpreters in Trials One and Four about how
to deliver the interpretation when the Deaf witness was on
the stand. This means that the interpreters split the interpreting process, with one interpreter providing the ASL to
English interpretation and the other interpreter providing
the English to ASL interpretation. Both interpreters monitored the accuracy of the work being produced by their
interpreting partner, and offered corrective information
when necessary in order to present an accurate message.

Trial Two: Notetaking
In Trial Two the interpreting team had reviewed during the preparation conversation how they would use notetaking strategies during the trial. The interpreters agreed

that they would note any facts and figures that might not be remembered easily, and they also wrote down the correct spelling of the names of the lawyers and witnesses. The interpreters agreed that during the expert witness testimony, the interpreter who was working in the support position would take notes, and feed the working interpreter the information if needed.

The notetaking materials were placed near the interpreters at all times. The notes were referred to once when spelling the witness's name.

Trial Two: Success Rate per Total Utterances

The three distinct events of this trial took one hour and forty minutes to complete. There were a total of 292 utterances during the expert witness testimony, 154 utterances during the direct evidence portion, and a total of 157 utterances during the cross-examination of the Deaf witnesses. The trial had an overall success rate of 98%.

Trial Two: Examples of Successful Interpretation

The following four examples demonstrate successful interpreting across each of three discourse events: expert witness, direct evidence and cross-examination. The patterns of success were very similar to the examples found in Trial One. The same writing conventions used in Trial One are used to present the examples for Trial Two.

1. Expert Witness Testimony

Witness: ...however, the fact that it is visual-gestural rather than aural-oral presents a number of differences in terms of how it conveys information. One way that it differs is its grammatical structure...

Interpreter: ASL MEANS WHAT? VISUAL-GESTUR-
AL LANGUAGE, NOT SPOKEN/HEAR
LANGUAGE. LANGUAGES DIFFER-
ENCES - MANY+++ HOW EXPRESS
INFORMATION DIFFERENT. EXAMPLE,
GRAMMAR DIFFER...

In this example the witness paused for the interpreter, allowing for natural "chunks" of information to be
conveyed. The interpreter successfully used a compare and
contrast strategy, and the use of space to compare ASL and
spoken languages. Each time the interpreter presented the
work, there was a specific reference to ASL.

2. Direct Evidence

Lawyer: And is your teacher in court today?

Interpreter: MS. HOWARD, TEACHER - WOOD
SHOP - YOU SEE HER IN COURTROOM
- HERE TODAY? SEE - POINT WHERE?

Interpretation had an equivalent message and has
incorporated all of the features successfully. What was
made explicit in the interpretation was the teacher's name
and the need for the witness to point to the accused, which
was the expected response in the original message. This
strategy builds cohesion at the discourse level of language,
and contributes to the overall cohesive effect of the
emerging text.

3. Cross-Examination

Lawyer: So you would agree with me that it really
              didn't hurt that much...

Interpreter: ME RIGHT YOU AGREE - HAMMER
              HIT HEAD HURT NOTHING, RIGHT -
              LIGHT, NOT HARD, HURT NOTHING.

The interpretation had an equivalent message and has incorporated all of the features of a successful message per the criteria used in the analysis of data.

4. Direct Evidence

Lawyer: For the record Sir, you have seen the witness
              indicate the size of the piece of wood.

Judge: Yes, it would appear that the measurement is
              approximately 1.5 feet in length.

Interpreter: (Shifts body away from witness)
              B-handshape - TALK BETWEEN TWO OF
              THEM....NOTICE...WOOD SIZE SHOW
              JUDGE: YES, SEEM SIZE 1.5 FEET
              LONG.

During this overlapping exchange between the judge and lawyer, the interpreter shifted her body, clearly indicating it was a conversation between the two parties, and interpreted the remarks. The work was successful per all linguistic and functional parameters and resulted in the witness acknowledging with an affirmative head nod that the judge was correct in his estimation of the size of the wood. This affirmative head nod was then interpreted as a spoken English utterance for the court record.

Trial Two: Error Rate per Total Utterances

In this trial, during expert witness testimony there were only five interpretation errors made. When direct evidence was entered, there were four errors in the English to ASL interpretation and one error in the ASL to English interpretation. Each question was presented via consecutive interpretation. On one occasion the interpreter chose to check his/her comprehension of the question with the team interpreter. The results are illustrated in Table 3.10.

There were no false starts and nor were there any occasions that the Deaf witness asked for the interpreter to repeat themselves. During the cross-examination, there was one error from English to ASL and no errors from ASL to English.

TABLE 3.10
Interpretation Errors by Ratio of Total
Utterances and Discourse Event: Trial Two

Discourse Event	Errors per Utterances	Percentage of Error (%)
Expert Witness	5/292*	2.35
Direct Evidence	4/154	2.6
Cross-Examination	1/157	.64
Total Trial Utterances	10/603	1.67

* Note: to be read as 5 errors out of 292 total utterances

In this second trial, a 98% accuracy rate was achieved by using consecutive interpreting strategies. The majority of errors in this trial occurred during direct evidence, with 3 errors in the ASL to English work and 1 error in the English to ASL work. During cross-examination, there was 1 error in the English to ASL work and no errors in the ASL to English work. This error rate is significantly lower than Trial One.

Trial Two: Examples of Unsuccessful Interpretation.
As noted in Table 3.10, there was a 1.67% error rate for this trial. As with Trial One, the following three examples are of a similar linguistic nature, in terms of omissions and additions of content, shifts in register, and ungrammatical ASL constructions.

1. Expert Witness Testimony

Witness: Deaf people typically use different head nods which mean different things. For example, this kind of headnod (witness demonstrating) can mean, "Yes, I am following you", but it doesn't mean "Yes, I am agreeing with you."

Interpreter: DEAF PEOPLE PAH HEAD NOD AND HEAD SHAKE MEAN SAME NOT. EXAMPLE - THAT (POINTS TO WITNESS, THEN USES CLASSIFIER TO REPRESENT HEAD NOD) - HEAD NOD. MEANS WHAT? YES, I UNDER STAND. NOT MEAN - AGREE, NOT THAT.

The error that occurred in this utterance was that the interpreter made an addition that was not present in the source message. They added "head shake", which is generally viewed as a negative response, while the witness was only dealing with non-verbal behaviour that can be confusing to non-signers when watching a Deaf person use it.

2. Direct Evidence

Witness: I DON'T PAY ATTENTION IN HIS
             CLASS. I'D RATHER CHAT WITH MY
             FRIENDS. TEACHER INTERESTING?
             NEVER! NEVER TEACHES ANYTHING
             OF INTEREST.

Interpreter: I do pay attention in class, but my friends
             get me to chat with them. The teacher isn't
             interesting at all.

The error here was one of misunderstanding the witness and saying the witness did pay attention, which was not present in the original message. As well, there was an interpreting skew when the answer was presented as, "...my friends get me to chat with them", whereas in the original message, the witness acknowledged that she would rather chat with her friends than pay attention.

3. Cross-Examination

Lawyer: Isn't it true that this wasn't the first time you
             were kicked out of that class, correct? In
             fact, you were suspended in February,

correct?

Interpreter: TRUE - FIRST TIME KICKED OUT -
NOT. HAPPEN LAST FEBRUARY,
KICKED OUT, TOO, RIGHT?

The error here was one of misunderstanding the term suspended, which was interpreted as "kicked out", which differed from the original message. The error was corrected by the Deaf witness who signed back:

Witness: KICKED OUT - YOU MEAN I WAS
SUSPENDED? THAT TIME?

This trial was conducted entirely by interpreters using consecutive interpretation for all segments of the trial, just as in Trial Two. The trial involved also three distinct aspects: the entering of expert witness testimony, with a non-deaf witness; the entering of Crown witness testimony, with a Deaf witness; and the cross-examination of the same Deaf witness by the defense attorney.

Trial Three: Error Patterns
Given how few errors were made in this trial, it cannot be said there were frequent and patterned errors. The individual errors included omissions and/or additions of content, and register inaccuracies when working from English into ASL.

Trial Three: Interpreter Preparation Strategies
This trial was like Trial Two in that it was conducted

using consecutive interpreting strategies. As with the first two trials, the two interpreters held a preparation conversation, in which they discussed their experience with courtroom work, how they prefer to receive corrective information and how to work as a team.

They agreed to split the expert testimony into two sections, with each interpreter providing interpretation for 20 minute segments. This in fact did not occur. The first interpreter continued to interpret the entire length of the testimony which lasted one hour and two minutes.

As in Trial One and Two, the interpreters were positioned identically throughout the discourse events. When the second interpreter was not actively interpreting, they were facing their interpreting partner, monitoring the accuracy of the work. In this trial, the support interpreter attempted to supply their colleague with information needed to provide an accurate message, but the working interpreter chose not to incorporate these cues. As a result, there were numerous errors found in the interpretation of the expert witness testimony.

The interpreters agreed to split the interpreting process for the Deaf witness testimony in the same manner as did the interpreters in Trials One and Two. Both interpreters monitored the accuracy of the work being produced by their interpreting partner, and offered corrective information when necessary in order to present an accurate message. This segment of the trial was more accurate than the expert testimony.

Trial Three: Notetaking

The interpreters did not address how notes could be used to support the interpreting in this trial. Nor did they put the available notetaking materials within their reach. As a result, one interpreter had to stop the courtroom proceedings and gather the notetaking materials needed. After that point, notes were used by the active interpreter during the expert witness testimony.

The notes were reviewed after the trial and they revealed that the interpreter adopted a word for word approach to notetaking. This strategy resulted in a very time consuming process that hindered the interpretation and overall dynamics of the situation, including turn-taking between participants. The form-based style of taking notes in English meant that the interpreter was not actively processing the message while hearing it. The English-based notes then added to the source language intrusions found in the interpreting. A preferred strategy would have been to use mapping or symbol based notetaking which would allow for the interpreter to focus on the meaning, and not be influenced by the grammar of the source language.

Trial Three: Success Rate per Total Utterances

Trial Three required two hours and twelve minutes to complete. There were a total of 353 utterances during the expert witness testimony, 193 utterances during the direct evidence portion, and a total of 188 utterances during the cross-examination of the Deaf witnesses. This trial had an overall success rate of 95%.

Trial Three: Examples of Successful Interpretation.

The following examples show successful interpretation across the three discourse events. As with Trials One and Two, the same reporting conventions have been used.

1. Expert Witness

    Witness: Because of the educational experiences that
                     some Deaf people have had, it may mean
                     that their abilities to read and write English
                     are substantially delayed.

    Interpreter: DEAF PEOPLE...EDUCATIONAL EXPE-
                     RIENCE VARY - ORAL, SIGNED
                     ENGLISH, ASL, MAINSTREAM, ETC,
                     MEANS WHAT? SOMETIMES DEAF
                     PEOPLE READ WRITE ENGLISH
                     DELAY   EQUAL HEARING NOT.

The example demonstrated the contextualization of the message regarding the educational experiences of deaf people. The use of four examples - oral, Signed English, ASL, and mainstream makes explicit what is conveyed in the words "educational experience". The message observed the grammatical features of ASL and effectively conveyed the affect and tone of the expert witness.

2. Expert Witness

    Witness: When I speak about name signs, that is a
                     convention used by Deaf people in ASL.
                     People who are known to the community are
                     assigned a name sign and that name sign can
                     be arbitrary or iconic.

    Interpreter: NAME SIGNS - WHO USE? DEAF PEO-
                     PLE PEOPLE USED ASL.   DEAF

> COMMUNITY WHO INVOLVED GIVE
> NAME SIGN. NAME SIGN CAN BE
> INVENT SAME AS A-R-B-I-T-R-A-R-Y
> OR CAN BE CHARACTERISTIC - LOOK
> LIKE THEM MEAN I-C-O-N-I-C.

The example demonstrated the message was processed at the semantic and sentential level. It was successfully restructured into ASL and included meaning based work, along with the specific English terms - arbitrary and iconic.

3. Direct Evidence

> Witness: IT'S MY PARENTS CABIN BUT THEY
> WERE IN HAWAII SO WE DECIDED TO
> GO THERE TO CELEBRATE NEW
> YEARS. WE HAD A GREAT DAY -
> USING SNOWMOBILES, RELAXING IN
> THE OUTDOORS.

> Interpreter: The cabin belongs to my parents who were
> in Hawaii at the time. We went to the cabin
> to celebrate New Years. The day was just
> great - we had spent it snowmobiling and
> just enjoying the outdoor weather.

In this example, the interpreter restructured the sentence structure to observe English conventions, while relaying the exact content. The tone and affect of the witness were accurately portrayed in this message.

4. Cross-Examination

    Lawyer: But, in fact you weren't paying any attention
                to your boyfriend, were you? You were too
                busy flirting with my client, isn't that true?

    Interpreter: BOYFRIEND - PAY ATTENTION - NOT!
                DO-DO? FLIRT+++ WITH WHO? JASON?
                RIGHT?

    In this example, the interpreter used a topic com-
ment structure in ASL to accurately deliver the content. The
interpretation conveyed the lawyer's affect and was successful in getting the witness annoyed which was demonstrated in the witness's response, which follows:

    Witness: IGNORE BOYFRIEND? NO. ME FLIRT
               WITH HIM (POINTS TO ACCUSED) - HA
               I NEVER EVEN SAW HIM. I WAS PLAY-
               ING CARDS, I ALREADY TOLD YOU
               THAT!

Trial Three: Error Rate per Total Utterances
    Table 3.11 describes the error rate per the number of
utterances for the trial, as separated by courtroom event, for
Trial Three.

TABLE 3.11
Interpretation Errors by a Ratio of Total
Utterances and Discourse Event: Trial Three

Discourse Event	Errors per Utterances	Percentage of Error (%)
Expert Witness	27/353*	7.6
Direct Evidence	6/193	3.1
Cross-Examination	3/188	1.6
Total Trial Utterances	36/720	5.0

* Note: To be read as 27 errors and 353 total utterances

In Trial Three a 95% accuracy rate was achieved by using consecutive interpreting strategies. The majority of errors in this trial occurred during expert witness testimony. During direct evidence there were 3 errors in the ASL to English work and 3 errors in the English to ASL work. During cross-examination, there were 2 errors in the English to ASL work and 1 error in the ASL to English work. The kinds of errors that emerged were similar to Trial One and Trial Two, and therefore the following section presents just two errors that may be more serious in nature.

Trial Three: Examples of unsuccessful work
1. Expert Witness

Witness: "...as in a courtroom, where often a series of questions are asked to narrow in on a

specific event or time frame....As the interpreter going into sign language I will have
to do a brief summation of that contextual
frame in order to pose the question and
"Then what happened?" sometimes that
is confusing because it seems that the interpreter is going on for so long, but it is a
linguistic necessity."

Interpreter: "...COURTROOM, QUESTIONS, QUES-
TIONS FOCUS ON SPECIFIC EVENT
TIME. ME INTERPRETER SIGNING
DO? (INTERPRETER STOPS WITNESS
- THEN CONTINUES) ...CAN BE CON-
FUSING BECAUSE INTERPRETER
INTERPRETS LONG TIME, BUT
NEED"

The errors that affected this segment included
numerous grammatical errors where the interpretation was
not presented in ASL but was delivered in English ordered
signing or contact-language. The interpreter was also
mouthing more English and the register switched from consultative in spoken English to casual in ASL. The interpreter stopped the witness mid-sentence and as a result the
work demonstrated omissions of content, specifically about
the contextual frame and linguistic necessity. Such work
does not accurately convey the testimony.

In the post-trial interview conducted with the Deaf
witness, they commented that they felt "lost" at this point in
the trial. They were unsure of whether it was the witness's
delivery or the interpreter's delivery that was problematic,

but as the event continued they indicated they "lost faith in the interpreter based on the work and dynamics they observed".

2. Expert Witness Testimony

Witness: If the witness was giving highly technical testimony, such a ballistic evidence or blood spatter analysis, you would anticipate that the interpreters would want to do that testimony via consecutive interpreting.

Interpreter: SUPPOSE WITNESS TALK ABOUT TECHNICAL - TECHNICAL COMPLICATED TOPIC, TRUE INTERPRETER TEND USE CONSECUTIVE.

In this example, the interpreter has omitted the topic reference and the specific details about ballistic evidence or blood spatter analysis, which leaves the message inaccurate per the source message. Such an abbreviated answer does not reflect the carefully chosen example of the witness and does not allow the Deaf consumer watching the interpretation to come to the same judgments about the metanotative aspects of the speaker.

Trail Three: Error Patterns

Despite the high level of accuracy of interpretation during the entering of direct evidence and the subsequent cross-examination, there were several aspects in this trial that caused problems. Specifically, the expert witness event

contained the greatest number of errors and unusual inter-
preter-created issues. For example, at one point Interpreter
A stopped the expert witness and asked her to repeat the
answer. Interpreter B simultaneously fed or cued the previous information in ASL to Interpreter A. Interpreter A held
up her hands as a gesture to stop the proceedings, looked at
Interpreter B, shook her head, and did not incorporate the
corrected information into the interpretation. Instead,
Interpreter A waited for the witness to repeat the answer.
This incident occurred at sixteen minutes into the trial suggesting that fatigue may have been a factor. During preparation, the interpreters had agreed to spell each other off at
twenty minutes, and to support each other by providing
information via ASL feeds. In this particular instance,
Interpreter A appeared to discount the information fed by
Interpreter B, and waited until the expert witness repeated
the answer. These decisions impacted negatively upon the
accuracy of the work, and drew attention to the interpreters.

Near the twenty minute mark, Interpreter B indicated that it was time to switch. Interpreter A shook her head
and continued to work. Interpreter B indicated four more
times that it was time to switch, and each time Interpreter A
responded by shaking her head, and on three occasions
signed "I'm okay" to the interpreter. These utterances were
not accessible to the lawyers and judge, although the Deaf
witness sitting in the body of the courtroom had access to
the information and was aware of the dynamics between the
two interpreters. At this point, the quality of interpretation
and trust between the team appeared to deteriorate.

Trail Three: Notetaking Strategies.
The time codes indicate that at twenty-seven

minutes into the expert witness testimony, the interpreters had not switched positions. Interpreter A asked permission to use a notepad and paper and began to write down the witness's remarks. This would have been a suitable decision had no team interpreter been present, but in this context a better decision would have been to have Interpreter B take the working position.

1. Word-for-word copying

When the notes were analyzed it was clear the interpreter was not using effective notetaking strategies, as there was an apparent word-for-word copying of the spoken English answer, as opposed to creating an interpretation map. An interpretation map is similar to a mind map and reflects a way for interpreters to hear the concepts, record the ideas without retaining the English source language form. This form of word-for-word notetaking also created longer time spans between hearing the witness's answer and providing the interpretation. The resulting interpretation had many source language intrusions and was presented in a form that often replicated the English grammar.

2. Pausing and Phrasing in the Target Language

As the expert witness testimony continued, the notes became more abbreviated and the work demonstrated greater accuracy in terms of content, grammar, register, affect and goal. Unfortunately, the pausing and phrasing was inconsistent in that the work was presented in linguistic form that was much slower than natural language pausing and phrasing, and there were four examples in which the interpreter had to repair utterances that s/he just interpreted. It was likely that fatigue was influencing the work at this time.

There were also examples of when a relatively short question asked by the lawyer had to be written down by the interpreter, as opposed to earlier in the interpretation when the interpreter was able to hear, comprehend, retain, and then offer the interpretation without relying on notes. For example:

Lawyer: So would that be the reason that many Deaf people wouldn't know who Perry Mason is?

Interpreter: (Behaviour: wrote down the entire question)...
I SEE - SO THAT REASON MANY DEAF PEOPLE DON'T KNOW WHO PERRY MASON?

Summary of Four Trials

This section has presented a quantitative analysis of each trial, which has illuminated both successful and unsuccessful segments of interpretation. The two trials which were interpreted using consecutive interpreting strategies showed a higher degree of accuracy as compared to the trials using simultaneous interpreting.

Based on an analysis of the four trials, there are some common patterns and strategies that contributed to the successful interpreting segments, including:

Preparation Strategies

When holding preparation conversations, the interpreters practiced the following strategies which contributed

to successful interpreting:
- Described how to work effectively as a team and came to agreements about how to share the work;
- Reviewed how notetaking could enhance successful interpretation;
- Addressed how they would handle errors and error correction;
- Reviewed signals that could be used to stop participants during consecutive trials; and
- Prepared the lawyers to work effectively with interpreters.

Interpreting Strategies

The following strategies also contributed to the provision of accurate interpreting:

- Interpreters switched at the 16-20 minute mark during expert witness testimony, which controlled for the fatigue factor in the work;
- Interpreters split the process of ASL to English interpreting and English to ASL interpreting during direct evidence and cross-examination. This permitted primary focus on one source language and one target language, versus two source languages and two target languages;
- Interpreters monitored each other's interpretation work and advised the court when an interpretation error had occurred prior to correcting it;
- Interpreters used increased processing time in simultaneous interpreting work which allowed for the deeper semantic meaning to be recognized,

which reduced the number of source language intrusions in the work and enhanced the accuracy of the interpretation;

- Supportive interpreter team behaviour presented a professional image to the Court and helped to build confidence in the interpretation;
- Consecutive interpreting was used for the direct evidence portion;
- Simultaneous interpreting was used for the cross-examination;
- Interpreters used pre-established signals to pause the witness, while nodding their head, indicating they had understood the message, but needed the witness to pause;
- Register and tone accurately reflected the speaker/signer;
- Politeness markers used by lawyers and judges were present in the interpretation;
- ASL grammar was consistently applied to the target messages;
- Interpreters used the same Size and Shape Specifier (SASS) or classifier as the Deaf witness, which told the Deaf consumer the interpreters had understood them;
- Complete thoughts were expressed in the target language of both ASL and English with consistent processing at the sentential level, as demonstrated by increased processing time;
- Ability to recognize and present speaker or signer goals in a manner that was suitable for the target language;
- Depth of processing strategies that allowed for

the explicit meaning, which was implied in the text, to be revealed;
- Use of compare and contrast grammatical features during the expert witness discourse event, which allowed for the analogies and metaphors of the source language to be interpreted into the target language; and
- Affectual components which represented the source language effectively in the target language.

The transcripts also revealed common errors patterns which included omissions, additions, shifts in register, form-based interpretation marked by many source language intrusions, and dysfunctional ASL grammar.

Summary

The results of the study indicated that there were significant differences between consecutive interpreting and simultaneous interpreting across three discourse events: expert witness testimony, direct evidence and cross-examination. Consecutive interpreting allowed for greater accuracy in interpreting across all three discourse events. There were more interpreting errors made during the expert witness testimony and during the entering of direct evidence than during cross-examination when using simultaneous interpreting.

The successful interpreting found in all four trials included all of the grammatical and functional features needed in order to offer an equivalent message. Specifically, the interpreters relied on the following strategies:

- Ability to recognize and present speaker or signer intentions in a manner that was suitable for the target language discourse frame;
- Depth of processing strategies that allowed for information implied in the text to be explicitly stated;
- Use of compare and contrast grammatical features during the expert witness discourse event, which allowed for analogies and metaphors of the sourcelanguage to be interpreted into the target language;
- Affectual components which represented emotive overlay in the source language were represented into the target language; and
- Ability to link ideas in the manner in which they were linked in the source language where grammatically possible.

CHAPTER 4

RESULTS: QUALITATIVE ANALYSIS

This chapter presents data obtained through audiotaping the preparation conversations held between interpreters, between interpreters and lawyers, and between interpreters and expert witness. In addition, semi-structured, open-ended interviews were conducted with all participants following the trials. The results of the preparation conversations are presented first, followed by the interview results.

Preparation Conversations

Chapter Two set out the four research objectives for this study, and Objective 3 was stated as: To investigate the preparation strategies of interpreters when working together as a team, when preparing lawyers about the task of working with interpreters, and when preparing with Deaf witnesses. The following section summarizes the results of the preparation conversations held between interpreters, between interpreters and lawyers, and interpreters and Deaf witnesses.

Interpreter Teams

Prior to each of the four trials, the interpreting teams working a given trial had an opportunity to prepare with each other. Conversations were audio recorded and the results analyzed for themes. The preparation questions that were most frequently discussed among the four teams are summarized as:

1. How best do we share this assignment?

The interpreters frequently reviewed how long the turns should be for each interpreter and whether they would split the interpreting process (ASL to English and English to ASL) during direct evidence and cross-examination.

2. How will I know when you need support or a feed?

In response to this question, the interpreters frequently discussed how the monitoring of accuracy of interpretation should take place, and how to offer corrective information if needed.

3. Do I feed you in ASL or English?

The interpreters also spoke of the specific language in which to offer cued information to their interpreting partner. Most often, the interpreters preferred to have information cued to them in ASL during the expert witness testimony, and in spoken English when interpreting direct evidence or cross-examination. The preferences were based on positioning, so that during expert witness testimony the interpreters were facing each other, and during direct evidence and cross-examination, the interpreters were standing next to each other.

4. Which one of us should speak to the lawyers involved?

Three of the interpreting teams decided to approach the lawyers as a team, and one interpreting team chose to identify a "primary spokesperson".

5. What information do we need/want to share?

The interpreters focused on the information they wanted to share with the lawyers, and the majority of the information related to the use of interpreters in the courtroom, specifics about signals and turn-taking, and specific descriptions of interpreting in simultaneous or consecutive interpreting modes.

6. What do we need the Court to do to make our work successful?

Again, the interpreters tended to focus on the strategies that lawyers could use to assist the interpreters, such as: speak at a normal speed, allow the interpreters to stop them if needed for clarification, and to ask one question at a time.

7. How much experience do you have with this type of trial?

The interpreting team used this question to exchange information about the degree of interpreting experience that each had with criminal trials involving sexual assault and assault. Two interpreting teams also commented on previous experience working with an expert witness.

When analyzing the trial data it would appear the following questions may have been helpful to the teams, yet they were not part of the preparation conversations:

1. How will we handle frozen text, such as oaths, in a consistent manner?

This question would have eliminated the problem that occurred in Trial Four and the multiple interpretations of the oath.

2. **What specific sign choices might we need for this assignment?**
   This question could have led to a discussion of the specific semantic choices needed in ASL and may have reduced the incidence of source language intrusions from spoken English into ASL.

3. **Have you met the witness before, and if so, what information would be helpful to me?**
   If one of the interpreters had met the witness(es) before, there may have been information that would assist the second interpreter in determining register, language use, topic range, and target language issues.

4. **What specific details of the case should we ask the lawyers to review with us?**
   This question could have led to further information that would have been helpful, for example, getting the scope of the expert witness testimony and the document that was entered as an exhibit.

5. **If we need to use notes during the trial, which one of us should take the notes? What notetaking symbols or structure would enhance the notes?**
   These questions may have helped the interpreter find a better system for creating notes as opposed to the word-for-word strategy that was used in Trial Three.

6. **Which one of us will tell the witness about the purpose of the notes and how they will be destroyed at the conclusion of the trial?**
   During the post-trial interview with Deaf witnesses, they expressed a need for the interpreters to have clarified this issue prior to using notes, based on a

sense that the notes might be taken from the court-room and seen by others. The witnesses comment-ed on the importance of confidentiality in all phases of the trial, and they saw the notes as one possible breach of confidentiality if not disposed of properly.

Interpreters Preparing with the Expert Witness

Three out of four interpreter teams held brief con-versations with the expert witness prior to the trials. In an interview with the expert witness after the conclusion of the trials, the following issues were raised:

- The expert witness was worried the team that did not take advantage of a preparation conversation would not understand the testimony. The witness indicated she had a reduced level of trust for the interpreting work of this team.
- Two teams prepared the witness by conducting the preparation conversation in a manner which focused on the needs of the interpreters to the exclusion of the needs of the witness. For example, the inter-preters stressed how they would be taking turns interpreting the testimony, how they would stop the witness during consecutive interpreting, the process they would use for correcting errors, and what they needed to do in order to present successful work. These are important features, but what is needed is an attempt to consider the goals of the witness, par-ticular evidence they want to highlight, etc.
- One team prepared with the witness by asking about the goals of the testimony. This strategy was appre-ciated by the witness, who felt more confident the interpreters would then be able to interpret the

content if they had a sense of overall goals or
schema.

- The witness had a resume and article ready to sub-
  mit to the Court. All of the interpreters focused on
  the resume details, but none asked to see the article
  to be submitted to the Court. In contrast, the article
  would have been more useful to the interpreters as it
  outlined every possible area of testimony to be
  given, and offered all of the examples that were used
  in the testimony.
- The witness is an experienced courtroom interpreter
  and as such was sometimes conscious of when to
  pause and wait for the interpreters to "catch up" during the trials. This would not be true of all expert
  witnesses and as such the interpreters would be
  required to be more assertive in stopping speakers in
  order to segment the messages when using consecutive interpreting.

Interpreters Preparing with Lawyers

The interpreters took time to prepare the lawyers for
working with interpreters and those conversations were also
audiotaped. The themes that emerged in the conversations
included the following:

1. Professionalism

   All lawyers commented on the professionalism of
   the interpreting teams during the trials. They suggested that the interpreters appeared more competent than many of the spoken language interpreters
   they had worked with in similar trials.

2. Describing interpreting work

Most of the lawyers indicated that the interpreters described the nature of their work in comprehensive and technical terms, but in a manner that was somewhat overwhelming. An example of a term they did not understand was "miscue", as opposed to saying, "If we make a mistake we will...". It would have been helpful to the lawyers if the interpreters had used examples or analogies when describing some terms about consecutive and simultaneous interpreting.

3. Content specific information

The majority of lawyers would have preferred that the interpreters ask more questions about the nature of the trial and specific elements that were key to the case.

One lawyer stated:

What is important to me is to feel confident in their interpreting skills and to know they understand the framework for the case. I am surprised interpreters don't ask more questions about that - we would give it to them if they asked.

4. Signals

All lawyers said they were sometimes confused by what signals the interpreters were planning to use in order to interrupt or pause the lawyers. This confusion resulted in some overlapping utterances between lawyers and interpreters, and some false starts during the question and answer of direct evidence and cross-examination.

5. Team processes

The lawyers understood that interpreters would sometimes need to confer with each other during the course of the trial, and this was covered in the preparation conversations; however, seven out of nine lawyers commented that they were not prepared for how frequently this would take place.

Post-Trial Interview Results

Interviews were held with all participants after the conclusion of the trials. The following summarizes the key themes which emerged from the interviews.

Lawyers

Overall, a great deal of satisfaction was expressed by the lawyers towards working with the interpreters. Consistently, the lawyers commented on their professional demeanor and their apparent fluency in American Sign Language (none of the lawyers can sign, and therefore they are not in a position to assess the accuracy or fluency, but they based this opinion on their perceptions of the trial process).

Lawyers indicated they had learned a great deal about working with Deaf people based on the experience, and that they would be interested in sharing this information with their colleagues.

The eight major themes which emerged, along with the related sub-themes are presented in Table 4.1.

TABLE 4.1
Interviews with Lawyers: Themes

Themes	Sub-Themes
Preparation	• Terminology • Trial Specific Details
Positioning	• Need to see the witness • Need to see the interpreters
Conferring	• Rationale for it • Frequency • Indicating to the Court when needed
Error Correction	• Language used to correct errors
Emotions	• Conveying affect of witness • Misreading Deaf witness's body language
Witness Control	• Lawyer control vs. interpreter control • Nodding seen as encouraging the witness
Simultaneous Interpreting	• Preferred method • Need for accuracy paramount
Consecutive Interpreting	• Build a case for use of consecutive • Cadence of cross-examination • Signals

Preparation

The lawyers appreciated the preparation conversations and suggested that the interpreters continue to perform this function. They noted that this has not been a consistent practice when working with spoken language interpreters and it is one that they viewed as helpful in building trust and confidence in the interpretation. A frequently reported response was:

> *I was surprised when they told us what they were doing. I have never worked with a signer before but the spoken language interpreters never tell us what they are doing! I appreciated this approach.*

The lawyers also felt that some of the interpreting terminology was new to them, and that it would have been helpful to have more examples or analogies to understand the relevance of using consecutive versus simultaneous.

Finally, the lawyers commented that the interpreters could have benefited from asking more trial specific questions, in order to establish a complete frame of reference.

Positioning

The lawyers wanted to be sure they could see the witness and sometimes their view was obstructed by the interpreters who were facing the Deaf witness, and therefore had their backs to the lawyers. The lawyers also commented that they would have preferred to see the interpreters while they interpreted even though they were not qualified to assess their work. There may have been some ways to restructure the courtroom environment but none of the interpreters or lawyers reviewed this in the preparation conversations. A frequently reported response:

> *I had never even thought about where the interpreters would need to be. When I work with foreign language interpreters we just need to make sure they can hear, but the signers have to able to see the Deaf person and vice versa - new for me. But, I didn't like having the interpreter's back to me.*

Conferring

During the preparation conversations, the interpreters described why they would need to confer or check with each other, in terms of monitoring the accuracy of the work, or clarifying an answer. While the lawyers understood this, some of them found the frequency with which this occurred to be a problem. They commented that it would have been helpful if the interpreters had indicated to the Court why they needed to confer prior to conferring.
One lawyer stated:

> *I started to wonder if they knew what they were doing. I felt concerned about how often it occurred and I didn't know why they were conferring with each other. Let me know the issue - I felt frustrated.*

Some of the lawyers felt the conferring interfered with their line of questioning. That sentiment is expressed in this quote:

> *I sometimes felt like I lost my train of thought when I was interrupted by the interpreters checking with each other. There needs to be a way to balance their over-analyzing the question to just allowing the question to stand.*

Error Correction

The lawyers frequently commented that they did not understand what an interpreter "miscue" was, and found that term less helpful than saying "interpreter error". Lawyers were primarily concerned with how the interpreters would correct errors, and some of the lawyers suggested they found it confusing at times to know if it was the witness changing their answer, or if it was an interpreter changing the information based on their own mistake.

Emotions

All of the lawyers expressed surprise at how effectively the interpreters were able to convey the emotions of the Deaf witness. In retrospect, they indicated that it would have been helpful for the interpreters to address this in their preparation session with the lawyers, because they had anticipated this to be an area of weakness in the interpretation. Given how unfamiliar the lawyers were in general with Deaf people, they identified a need to feel confident that the interpreters could accurately convey the affect of the witness.

They also commented on their own inaccurate perceptions:

> *It's a good thing we had the expert witness, or I may have misunderstood some of the facial expressions of the Deaf witness as anger or stressing a point that wasn't actually being stressed. I have always thought I was quite good at reading a witness but this situation showed me that I am not!*

Witness Control

Two lawyers felt uncomfortable with how the questioning process was interrupted by the interpreters, who on occasion would ask a witness to repeat an answer. The lawyers agreed that it was critical to them that they control the witness and that every action taken by an interpreter to interfere with the process was viewed negatively.

The lawyers also were confused about the need for interpreters to display attending behaviours when working with a Deaf witness, in spite of hearing expert testimony on this matter. They observed that on more than one occasion they saw the interpreters nodding while a witness was presenting an answer, and they questioned this behaviour. None of the lawyers understood the need to provide this sort of visual feedback to Deaf witnesses in order to let them know the interpreters are comprehending the message.

One lawyer summarized his feeling about this topic:

When I saw the interpreter nodding at the witness I thought immediately - they aren't being neutral, but instead were encouraging the witness to describe more of the events, and offering support to the witness. I have had sign interpreters working in trials before and I have never seen that - so when do they nod and when don't they?

Once again, this linguistic behaviour is one that could have been discussed in a preparation conversation.

Simultaneous interpreting

By far, the majority of lawyers preferred simultaneous interpreting. They felt it was faster and allowed for the case to proceed smoothly. When presented with the evidence of errors in simultaneous interpreting, all lawyers commented that accuracy was of paramount importance to them versus the speed of the trial, but that they lacked awareness of these issues prior to this experience. A frequently reported response:

I had never worked with a signing interpreter before, so I was pleased when I saw that they could keep up with my pace and sign at the same time as I was speaking. That worked really well.

Given the evidence after the trials about accuracy, they indicated that it is critical that the interpreter "build a case" to support the need for both consecutive and simultaneous practices in the courtroom.

Consecutive interpreting

While the lawyers were open to the use of consecutive interpreting for the expert witness testimony and for direct evidence, none of the defense lawyers liked using it during cross-examination. They all expressed frustration with how the consecutive interpreting put their cadence off, and how it was more challenging to put a witness "off their center" when there was so much time built into the question and answer period. The lawyers also suspected the additional time allowed the witness to be calmer than might normally be expected and allowed them more time to reflect on their answers.

Judges

As with the lawyers, the judges expressed a great deal of satisfaction with the interpreters and how the trials proceeded. Consistently, the judges commented on the interpreters' professional demeanor and apparent fluency in American Sign Language (none of the judges can sign, and therefore they are not in a position to assess the accuracy or fluency, but they based this opinion on their perceptions of the trial process).

All judges indicated they had learned a great deal about working with Deaf people based on the experience, commenting specifically on how helpful it was to hear the testimony of the expert witness. The judges suggested that this type of orientation should be made regularly available to members of the bar and bench.

The seven major themes which emerged from the interviews with the judges, along with the related sub-themes are presented in the following table.

TABLE 4.2
Interviews with Judges: Themes

Themes	Sub-Themes
Orientation	• Interpreting vs. transcoding • Reliability of interpreting • Need for two interpreters
Positioning	• Consecutive interpreting vs. narrative style • Need to see the witness • Need to see the interpreters
Conferring	• Rationale for it • Seeking permission first
Error Correction	• Language used to correct errors
Witness Control	• Nodding seen as encouraging the witness • Asking permission for rephrasing
Deafness	• Orientation • Assessment of credibility • Danger of assumptions
ASL	• Language differences • ASL fluency of Deaf witnesses

Orientation

The judges identified that it would be very helpful for the Bench to have an orientation provided similar to the information provided by the expert witness. Given the low incidence of deafness, they commented that it is rare for a judge to have a deaf participant in their courtrooms. Without current knowledge about deafness, ASL and interpreting issues, the judges are at risk of applying their own assumptions to the case at hand. For instance, the judges all assumed prior to the trials that the interpreters were providing a word-for-word equivalent "translation", based on their assumption that ASL has the same structure as English. Information on interpreting and some of the linguistic features of ASL was very new to the judges and helped to dispel some of their own myths about sign language and interpreting, but they recognized that their learning was only just beginning. Their suggestion was for printed information, which could be supplemented by further testimony in very serious matters.

A frequently reported response included:

That article the Crown entered, written by the expert witness was excellent. I learned a great deal from it, and would suggest that you create a similar document that can be given to all judges. Very, very helpful...

The judges also stated that it was crucial for the interpreters to be able to establish the reliability of their interpreting, and to succinctly address their qualifications, experience, and approach to error management. The need for two interpreters was also not well understood by the judges, who identified the need for orientation material and/or the interpreters to address these issues.

One judge commented that he had served in aboriginal communities and based on that experience had learned to adjust the questioning style in order to allow a more culturally appropriate narrative style to be used in the courtroom. The judge further wondered if the consecutive style of interpreting might have hindered a narrative style in ASL that might more closely approximate some of the native languages. His comments follow:

> *I wonder if it might have been better to just ask the witness to tell their story - much like we do in some cases with aboriginal people.*
>
> *I sensed the witness wanted to say much more than was in the answer.*
>
> *Does the questioning style, and then consecutive interpreting on top of that, impede their linguistic style?*

Positioning

In one of the trials, the judge stopped the proceedings to ask the interpreters to move behind the expert witness so that he could see them and also see the witness. This theme was also critical for the lawyers. The issue of positioning is also important for Deaf participants, and yet none of the preparation conversations addressed it. Judges commented that they want to observe the interactions between interpreters and witnesses, regardless of whether they understand the language.

Conferring

Prior to the trials the interpreters addressed the lawyers, but did not address the judges. It was during these preparation conversations that the interpreters described why they would need to confer or check with each other, in terms of monitoring the accuracy of the work, or clarifying an answer. The judges commented on the fact that they would have preferred the Crown prosecutors to review some of these basic interpreting behaviours with them prior to the commencement of the trial. While the judges could understand the need for the conferring, they also recommended that the interpreters always seek permission prior to conferring, and to indicate why they are conferring with each other. If the conferring takes more than a few seconds, the judges would rather the questions/answer be repeated, and they would prefer that they direct that interaction, not the interpreters.

Error correction

The judges were very concerned about the accuracy of interpretation, and how errors would be identified and corrected. They had various suggestions about how that should be phrased, but the common theme was that the interpreters should use language that makes it clear on the official record that it was an interpreter error and then offer the correct information. They, like the lawyers, commented that they did not understand what a "miscue" meant in the context of errors.

> *In my courtroom I want the interpreters to be very clear about when there has been an error made and the record needs to show the correction. The team who clearly said: Interpreter error, and then corrected it - well, I thought that worked extremely well. I wish some of the spoken languag interpreters would do the same.*

<u>Witness control</u>

The judges had a different perception than the lawyers when commenting on witness control. The judges observed that the interpreters had consistently asked for the judge to direct lawyers to rephrase or repeat a question.

The judges and lawyers agreed about the need for interpreters to make the Court aware of the need to display attending behaviours when working with a Deaf witness. They observed that on more than one occasion they saw the interpreters nodding while a witness was presenting an answer, and they questioned this behaviour. Like the lawyers, the judges did not understand the need to provide this sort of visual feedback to Deaf witnesses in order to let them know the interpreters are comprehending the message. Their interpretation of the interpreter's "nodding behaviour" was that of encouraging the witness to say more and expressing agreement with the witness.

<u>Deafness</u>

After hearing the expert witness testimony, the judges were consistent in their comments that stressed the need for information about deafness. They pointed to how important it is for them to assess the credibility of witnesses, and they identified that their standard approaches may not work with a Deaf witness. For example, the judges commented on how they misunderstood the non-manual behaviours of Deaf witnesses, which are linguistic features of ASL, and yet were misconstrued as emotions. They also did not understand how a Deaf witness could shake their head "negatively" and yet in the interpretation express an affirmative answer, until after they heard the expert witness testimony.

They also identified the danger of assumptions about the nature of deafness in general, from lipreading, educational levels and opportunities, the importance of communication that is accessible to deaf people, and so on. Again, the judges suggested that much of this information could come in the form of printed information, supplemented by educational seminars offered to judges at their yearly conferences.

ASL

The judges were astounded at the differences in the language structure of ASL and how that could affect interpreting in the courtroom. They also commented on how the information on ASL has prompted them to question the interpreting performed for some other minority language forms. Said one judge:

> *If it is this complicated in American Sign Language, what happens in some of the Eastern block languages we are seeing in Calgary courts?*

Additionally, the experience has caused one judge to question how the Court can confirm that the Deaf witness is fluent in ASL in order to ensure they understand the interpreters.

Finally, the judges commented on the need to build in extra time when working with Deaf witnesses and interpreters, and how important it is for them to be prepared if working trials that involve Deaf people. They also confirmed that they would support the need for videotaped trials involving serious matters with Deaf participants, which was not something they had ever considered prior to this experience. Like the lawyers, they recognized that original testimony given in ASL would have to be videotaped if there was the potential for an appeal.

Deaf Witnesses

The Deaf witnesses commented on the trials from the perspective of being able to "tell their story" and how effective the interpreting was in allowing them complete access to the courtroom content and processes.

Interestingly, the Deaf witnesses expressed the most comfort with the interpreter with the least amount of courtroom experience. That particular interpreter was viewed as the most "fluent and natural user of ASL", and presented the interpretation with confidence and completeness. There was strong agreement between the Deaf witnesses that this interpreter presented the information consistently in ASL which created a sense of comfort and trust between witness and interpreter. The witnesses noted that this interpreter also demonstrated the greatest sensitivity to the Deaf witness's emotional state when preparing for the trials, by not asking a number of specific details, but rather by engaging in social conversation. Through this social conversation, the Deaf witnesses felt confident that the interpreter would understand their messages and would be able to represent their "voice" in the courtroom.

The major themes which emerged from the interviews with the Deaf witnesses, along with the related sub-themes, are presented in Table 4.3.

TABLE 4.3
Interviews with Deaf Witnesses: Themes

Themes	Sub-Themes
Courtroom Protocol	• Unfamiliar environment • Questioning styles • Identifying who is speaking • Interpreter created utterances
Interpreting	• Consecutive • Simultaneous • ASL • Matching consumer style
Conferring	• Purpose - was I not clear? • Effect on witness
Error Correction	• Identifying errors and correction • Back translation of corrections
Interpreter behaviour	• Nervousness • Team processes
Notetaking	• Purpose • Disposal of notes
Preferences	• Confident interpreter • No hesitations • Nervousness at minimum • Collegial behaviour

Courtroom protocol

Both Deaf witnesses stated that the courtroom can be a very intimidating situation for them, and one where they are acutely aware of their minority language status. Based on this unfamiliarity, they expressed the need for the interpreters to be confident in these settings.

Part of the protocol that was unfamiliar to the witnesses was the questioning style used by the lawyers. For example, both Deaf witnesses wanted to tell their "whole story" in ASL and then have the lawyers ask them questions, but that is not how a trial proceeds. They suggested that one of the interpreter strategies that they found most effective was when the interpreters were able to be very explicit about the lawyers' questions. Said one witness:

When the interpreter made it clear WHAT the questions meant, then I felt confident I was answering what was expected. I didn't want to feel out of place, but I just wasn't sure sometimes what the question meant. I am sure the lawyer was clear, so I need the interpreter to be clear, too.

They also suggested that they are unfamiliar with why and how a judge may intervene during testimony, and as such, they stated that it is critical that interpreters indicate who is speaking at any given time, and when the conversation does not directly involve them.

The Deaf witnesses commented that they were aware that sometimes the interpreters were speaking to judges, lawyers, or to each other but this information was not always was made accessible to them. Some interpreting teams were consistent in working as a team to make sure that interpreter created utterances were interpreted while other teams were less consistent. It is the consistency that builds confidence and truly allows for all the courtroom discourse to be accessible to Deaf witnesses.

Interpreting

The Deaf witnesses each experienced one trial using consecutive interpreting and one trial using simultaneous interpreting. Both witnesses found the consecutive to be time consuming but noticed a marked improvement in the ASL grammar used by the interpreters when the work was processed consecutively. Their observations were that the interpreters had fewer false starts, were able to sign the statement or question accurately the first time and the Deaf consumer understood the intent and nuances behind the questions when the interpreters fully processed the information.

The one witness who has worked frequently as a Deaf interpreter (paired with an non-deaf interpreter, the Deaf interpreter provides linguistic and cultural interpretation that meets the Deaf consumer's needs) in courtrooms was more comfortable with the consecutive processes and much more aware of the impact of consecutive on accuracy of work. The other witnesses indicated they had always made the assumption that interpreters who worked simultaneously were "much better" interpreters. By participating in the study, both witnesses stated they have a much clearer sense of the interpreting process and some of the linguistic challenges presented in a courtroom. Both witnesses observed that the interpreters seemed unsure sometimes when to stop a witness in order to "chunk" the message. They compared this to other interpreting scenarios where they had experienced interpreters using a "shorter chunking pattern" with more effective results.

Both witnesses found it disturbing that at times when they were trying to be evasive in their answers that the interpreters would assume they had misunderstood and ask for the answer to be repeated. As one witness said:

> *My goal was to be vague and specifically not provide a detailed response to the lawyer's question. Leave it to the lawyer to probe more and be confused by my answer. The interpreter should not control this process.*

Conferring

Both Deaf witnesses could understand when the interpreters needed to clearly understand a lawyer's question or comment and how that could result in the interpreters conferring with each other. However, they did not understand why the interpreters needed to confer on ASL to English answers that the witnesses felt they had clearly expressed. They indicated the impact of the conferring behaviour was such that it made them less confident about the interpreter's receptive skills and more conscious of trying to produce very clear answers. They also commented that when the conferring went on for what seemed like "a very long time", they would have preferred to just repeat their answer. In one trial, the Deaf witness observed a strategy that was effective in building confidence and offering an inclusive experience for the Deaf person. In that situation, the team of interpreters conferred on an ASL to English answer, and once they agreed upon the answer, as Interpreter A was presenting the message in spoken English, Interpreter B represented the spoken English in ASL so the Deaf witness knew what the interpreters had voiced. This ensured the Deaf witness was included and had access to all of the information that came out of the conferring process. The Deaf witness indicated that this built confidence in that the interpretation was accurate and that all of the details were in the correct order as per the original answer.

Error correction

As with lawyers and judges, the Deaf witnesses were concerned that errors would not be identified and corrected. They appreciated the interpreters who indicated when it was an interpreter mistake but they were confused when lawyers were directed by the judge to rephrase a question. When this rephrasing occurred, they assumed it was because of an interpreting error, and hence suggested that the interpreters needed to "metacomment" prior to offering the new question. For example, the interpreters could have added in ASL:

> *"Judge has ordered the lawyer to change question, here is the new question..."*

A frequently reported response from the Deaf witnesses was:

> *How a Deaf person comfortably follows courtroom proceedings is tied to their feeling of being an equal participant. When I know what we are doing, why we are stopping, why a question was rephrased – especially during my testimony, well, I feel that I can tell my story. When I am lost, I don't think I come across clearly, and then the Court won't believe me...*

Interpreter behaviour

For all of the trials, the Deaf witnesses commented on some of the interpreters who appeared nervous. The Deaf witnesses wondered why the interpreters were nervous in that they were experienced interpreters, familiar with the setting. From the Deaf perspective, the frequent response was:

> *I should be the one to be nervous - not the interpreters!*

Both Deaf witnesses observed that when the interpreter appeared nervous it affected the witness negatively, and created a sense of anxiety for the Deaf witness. Their recommendation to the interpreters was:

> *They need be "warmed up" (in ASL) prior to the start of court, and to try not to show their nervousness. It is like any job - relax and interpret...*

One of the most important aspects raised by both witnesses was that the interpreters must function both professionally and as a team. The one witness who experienced the team of interpreters who did not split the work of the expert witness testimony was disturbed by the lack of professionalism and the resulting dynamics between the two interpreters. Again, this witness commented that the interpreters' behaviour influenced them, and made them wary of other decisions the team would make during direct evidence or cross-examination.

Notetaking

Interpreters who relied on notetaking strategies during the trials were viewed positively by the Deaf witnesses, but they observed that they would have preferred the interpreters raise this topic in the preparation conversation. For example, they suggested the interpreters identify the purpose of the notes and let the witness know the notes would be handed to the court clerk for disposal at the end of the trial.

One of the Deaf witnesses felt the notetaking of the expert witness testimony took far too long and created more attention to the interpreting process than necessary. This witness suggested the interpreter use a form of shorthand to speed up the process, which is expressed in the following quote:

> *I think they learn how to take notes in the inter-preing program. Maybe these interpreters need to learn that, too - because they need a shorthand way to do it...not write every word down.*

Preferences

Overall, both witnesses identified that it was crucial for them to have interpreters who demonstrated the following skills and abilities:

- Fluency in ASL;
- Ability to show the English to ASL interpretation confidently and without hesitation;
- Ability to control their own nervousness;
- Respect for everyone including their team mate, the lawyers and judge;
- Recognition of "control" boundaries in the courtroom, i.e., not appear to take control of the courtroom but rather negotiate what would be appropriate without bringing undue attention upon the Deaf witness.

Expert Witness

The expert witness had unique observations, based on experience as a courtroom interpreter providing consecutive and simultaneous interpreting, and as the witness educating the Court about interpreting and deafness related issues.

The five major themes which emerged from the interview with the expert witness, along with the related sub-themes, are presented in Table 4.4.

TABLE 4.4
Interviews with Expert Witness: Themes

Themes		Sub-Themes
Preparation	•	Content
	•	Interpreter needs
	•	Witness goal
	•	Confidence in interpretation
Interpreting	•	Consecutive
	•	Simultaneous
	•	Chunking of messages
Positioning	•	Visibility to all
Interpreter behaviour	•	Nervousness
	•	Team processes
Notetaking	•	Strategies
	•	Tools

Preparation

The witness observed that three out of the four teams chose to prepare in advance of the trial. In two of those preparation conversations, the focus was on what the interpreters needed and very little focus was on the proposed content. One team focused the preparation conversation on the goal of the testimony, which allowed the witness to explore areas of their testimony and the overall discourse schema to deliver that information. The expert witness indicated greater comfort with this latter approach to preparation, and hence had more confidence in that interpreting team. The witness suggested that the questions focused on witness academic qualifications were important, but that the interpreters did not ask enough questions about the areas of testimony. This may be because the interpreters assumed they would understand it easily because of the topic area, however the number of errors found in the interpretation of the expert witness testimony does not support this assumption.

The witness also submitted a document to the Court and this document would have helped the interpreters with potential questions and answers. However, none of the interpreters asked if any documents were going to be entered as evidence or if they could peruse them prior to the trial. The witness commented that if the interpreters had possessed solid training in the use of consecutive interpreting it would have likely improved their simultaneous interpreting. As identified earlier, all the interpreters indicated they used consecutive interpreting in their regular practice, but none of them had formal training in its use.

Interpreting

The expert witness, like the Deaf witnesses, commented on how the interpretation appeared more accurate and was easier to understand when it was provided consecutively. However, the witness observed that the interpreters seemed to stop the witness at inappropriate times as opposed to at the completion of a thought or idea. It appeared to the expert witness that the interpreters were not using appropriate chunking strategies to divide the responses, so that the interpreters would either stop the witness too soon, or wait far too long, and then have to ask for aspects to be repeated as they may have forgotten portions of the answer.

The witness offered this comment:

When working consecutively, we (as interpreters) need to hear enough of the message to understand it, and have a complete thought or linked thoughts, so that we can produce the message. We also need to know when our memory capacity is full, so that we can predict how long of a response we can take...it is a balancing act that comes with plenty of experience using consecutive.

The witness observed that when the interpreters were providing simultaneous interpretation from ASL to English, there were more false starts and repairs than when compared to the consecutive delivery. Additionally, when the interpreters utilized more processing time in their simultaneous work, they were able to produce more meaning-based interpretation.

Positioning

The expert witness, like the judges and lawyers,

commented on the positioning of the interpreters. During one trial, prior to the judge asking the interpreters to move, the interpreters were standing in front of the witness box, which felt very intrusive to the witness. The witness felt that she did not have the complete attention of the judge or lawyers when that particular position was chosen. Once the interpreters were placed slightly behind her, she was able to see the judge and lawyers better and felt a more direct communication pattern emerged.

Interpreter behaviour

The expert witness observed that the interpreters' sense of nervousness may have been heightened knowing that they were working with this particular expert who is well known in the interpreting field and who could also understand the interpretation provided in the courtroom. The witness indicated that she attempted not to monitor their work while giving testimony but suggested she should have indicated this explicitly during the preparation conversations as this may have reduced the interpreters' nervousness.

The expert witness, like the Deaf witnesses, was disturbed by the breakdown in teamwork in Trial Three during the expert witness testimony. The witness believed that many of the interpreting errors would not have taken place if the interpreters had switched. The fatigue of working a 60 minute segment alone sets the interpreter up for failure and was easily avoidable. The witness commented:

> *It would be interesting to know what the interpreters were thinking at that time that caused them to make the decision they did. Interpreters must recognize their limits and work with the supports*

available to them - for example, their colleague was ready to replace them. Was this about their own need to appear in control? I am not sure, but it certainly didn't reflect well upon the team.

The resulting discomfort between the two interpreters was obvious to the witness, who then assumed that the lawyers and judges may have detected the team breakdown as well.

Notetaking

The witness commented on the one interpreting team's lack of foresight when preparing for the testimony. For example, the interpreter did not have pen and paper ready to take notes, but rather had to stop the proceedings in order to request the materials. Based on the witness's own experience using consecutive interpreting and taking notes, it was clear to the witness that the interpreter was not using effective notetaking strategies as the interpreter was taking too long to record information, and then interpret the same information. Strategies and tools, such as producing discourse maps and using symbols, frequently used by spoken language interpreters would have enhanced the notetaking strategies and reduced the impact of source language intrusions.

Interpreters

The interpreters were invited to reflect on their work and the experience through the interview process. The major themes which emerged from the interviews with the interpreters, along with the related sub-themes, are presented in Table 4.5.

TABLE 4.5
Interviews with Interpreters: Themes

Themes		Sub-Themes
Preparation	•	Content
	•	Interpreter needs
	•	Effective strategies: witnesses and lawyers
Interpreting	•	Consecutive
	•	Simultaneous
	•	Chunking of messages
Courtroom discourse	•	Keeping up with pace/complexity
	•	Nervousness
	•	Impact of discourse style
Team Building	•	Team work
Processes	•	Trust in colleagues
Notetaking	•	Strategies
	•	Materials ready

Preparation

All participants were clear on their perspectives that there was additional content-specific information that they should have reviewed with each other during the preparation conversations. Upon reflection they expressed concern that they had spent too much time on examining what was needed in order for the interpreting to go well, and not enough time dealing with the specific content of the trial. An example raised was how obtaining the document from the expert witness would have helped them during the testimony but they had not thought to ask about it. The majority of interpreters recognized they needed to add more questions to their preparation conversations, especially when dealing with the lawyers.

<u>Interpreting</u>

The interpreters commented on their use of consecutive and simultaneous interpreting, and assessed the quality of their interpretation when using one mode over the other. The majority of interpreters recognized that their work was more successful and accurate when provided consecutively but said that it sometimes felt unnatural to them given the common practice of using simultaneous interpreting. All interpreters commented that they needed additional training in notetaking and chunking of information when using consecutive interpreting processes, which was not part of their formal interpreter training. Prior to the trials, all the interpreters had indicated experience with consecutive interpreting. One of the interpreters also emphasized that consecutive interpreting was what she used always in courtroom settings.

<u>Courtroom Discourse</u>

The interpreters acknowledged that when they felt the pressure of time during the trials, they wanted to use the simultaneous mode in order to "keep up with the volume", even though they recognized their work was less processed and used fewer ASL grammatical principles when interpreted simultaneously. The interpreters viewed their nervousness as representative of their regular work in a courtroom, in that when the pace of the trial increases and discourse becomes more complicated they feel anxious about the interpreting.

The interpreters also viewed the discourse style of the lawyers as a significant feature that influenced their work. One interpreter commented:

When the lawyer style was animated and lively, I had an easier time understanding their points and arguments. For the lawyers who were slow speakers, and were monotone, I had more difficulty following their courtroom style.

One interpreter noted that the interpreters can use this type of discourse to determine whether to use a consecutive or simultaneous mode of interpreting.

I realized after the trial was done simultaneously that there were places I would have liked to use consecutive interpreting. Like during the expert witness testimony, there were places I needed far more lag time to process the meaning. A blend of consecutive and simultaneous would have fit well for that particular discourse style.

Team Building Processes

All interpreters were asked about their view of working effectively as a team. Interpreters assessed their strategies for dealing with witnesses and lawyers and seemed comfortable with the approach they took to spelling each other in twenty minute segments for the expert witness testimony and splitting the interpreting process for Deaf witnesses. All teams commented on the fact that when there was "synergy" between the team members, they functioned effectively and created successful interpretation.

The interpreters assigned to Trial Three commented that during the preparation, one interpreter acknowledged s/he were somewhat anxious as s/he had limited courtroom experience. This was seen by the more experienced interpreter as an indication the interpreter was less capable. This also influenced the more experienced interpreter's decision not to switch during the entire expert witness testimony. This incident led to frustration between the two interpreters, along with feelings of anger and a sense of power imbalance. For the Deaf witness, this incident led to a feeling of mistrust of the interpreting team and elevated anxiety when giving their own testimony. Had the interpreter honored the original agreement, and if the second interpreter had been more professionally assertive, this incident would not have occurred. The Trial Three team commented on their struggle to work together and how much that affected the quality of interpretation, with one interpreter saying:

> *I am so uncomfortable about how we handled that.*
> *I realize I should have trusted you more...but form-*
> *ing a team takes time. I generally work on my own*
> *or with my set interpreting partners. We have never*
> *worked together and I thought that we would be*
> *able to work fine, but I guess team work is more than*
> *just being placed together and having a short con-*
> *versation before the assignment. You are certified -*
> *there was no reason for me to doubt your skills.*

Notetaking

All interpreters indicated that they could benefit from specific training in notetaking strategies and discourse mapping as tools to enhance their interpreting work. All four interpreters indicated that they do not frequently take notes in the course of their work, nor have they ever had

training in this area, either in their basic interpreter education program or through professional development workshops. Interpreter discourse maps and notetaking strategies
are part of many current interpreter education curricula but
none of these interpreters have been exposed to the
approaches.

Again, the interpreters assigned to Trial Three commented they should have had the materials ready for use,
instead of stopping the entire courtroom proceedings to get
the materials.

> *I am so embarrassed I had to stop the Court. I*
> *don't know why I forgot to have the materials*
> *ready...oh, that was a good lesson for me!*

The interpreters commented that this is an area of
professional development that hasn't been taught, and that
they need to learn more about notetaking. One interpreter
commented that this may be an area where spoken language
and sign language interpreters could collaborate and hold
joint workshops since it has always been part of the practice
of spoken language interpreters.

Summary

The data from the personal interviews supported and
clarified the results of the trials and allowed for multiple
perspectives on the experience to be documented.

CHAPTER 5

DISCUSSION OF THE RESULTS

This chapter first discusses the results of the study
as it provides information on the research objectives set out
in Chapter Two. Next, the study is critically reviewed by
examining the contributions, implications and limitations.
Finally, directions for future research are proposed.

Simultaneous versus Consecutive

The first research question pertained to the differen-
tial effectiveness of simultaneous interpretation and consecutive interpreting when dealing with three courtroom discourse events. Quantitative and qualitative data provide
insight into this research question. The quantitative results
of this study demonstrated that consecutive interpreting
allowed for a greater degree of interpreting accuracy. The
analysis of four mock trials showed the two trials in which
consecutive interpreting was used produced a higher degree
of interpreting accuracy, 98% and 95% respectively, compared to the trials where simultaneous interpreting was
used, which demonstrated accuracy rates of 83% and 87%.

Alexieva (1991), Bruton (1985) and Mikkelson
(1995) found that consecutive interpreting results in greater
accuracy in the transmission of message when working
between spoken languages, and this research shows a similar result with ASL and spoken English.

Tests of Significance conducted using a chi square

analysis of the type of interpreting (consecutive and simultaneous) across the three discourse events demonstrated a statistically significant association between the error rate and the type of interpretation. These three tests of significance demonstrated that the consecutive mode of interpretation was more accurate than the simultaneous mode of interpretation, across all three discourse samples.

The results of the two trials using consecutive interpreting demonstrated fewer error rates for all three discourse events when compared to simultaneous interpreting. All four trials indicated the lowest rate of errors in the cross-examination event.

When dealing with the expert witness testimony, conducted using simultaneous interpreting, Trial One had a 10% error rate and Trial Four had a 15.8% error rate. This can be contrasted with trials using consecutive interpreting, Trials Two and Three, which had error rates of 2.35% and 7.6% respectively. Using this same framework of contrasting simultaneous and consecutive interpreting, the direct evidence event is examined next. Trials One and Four had similar rates of errors: Trial One had an error rate of 21% and Trial Four had an error rate of 24.3%. During the consecutively interpreted trials (Trial Two and Three) the error rates for direct evidence were 2.6% and 3.1% respectively. Finally, when comparing the error rates for the cross-examination framework, Trials One and Four demonstrated error rates of 8% and 9.7%, while the consecutive trials demonstrated the following: Trial Two had an error rate of .64% and Trial Three had a 1.6% error rate.

While all aspects of a trial are of importance, the area of giving direct evidence and the subsequent cross-examination is critical. Given the results, there appears to be a need to address the errors and to reduce them by using interpreting strategies appropriate to the discourse frame. If Deaf people are to have access to the legal system via accurate interpreting services, it would appear that consecutive interpreting allows for the most accurate rendition of direct evidence. Further, with the error rates demonstrated in this study, the courts may feel more confident that Deaf witnesses are able to relay their experiences completely and accurately to the court via consecutive interpreting.

During Trial Three, which was conducted using consecutive interpreting, there were a greater number of errors when compared to Trial Two which was also conducted using consecutive interpreting. The unusual circumstances that arose during the expert witness testimony contributed to the higher rate of interpreting errors. In this trial, the two interpreters did not switch or spell each other off, which meant that one interpreter worked an hour long segment. The issues of fatigue and the style of notetaking appear to have contributed to the higher number of errors that were exhibited in this segment.

Qualitative information was also useful to examining the first research question. Material from the post-trial interviews was informative in regard to what constitutes accuracy and how it is best achieved when using simultaneous or consecutive interpreting. Of particular interest was the area of error management and discourse analysis, which are discussed in the following sections.

Error Management

The interpreters worked in teams of two and prior to

the trials, they engaged in preparation work. Part of their preparation discussions focused on how to manage errors should errors be made. When interpreters spoke to lawyers prior to the trials, all four teams emphasized the strength of having two interpreters working a trial. Their rationale was this: The ability of the support interpreter to monitor the accuracy of the working interpreter ensures the interpreting is accurate. Despite this arrangement there were numerous errors that were not corrected during witness testimony.

This is of concern in that the witnesses, lawyers and judges have no way to assess the accuracy of the interpretation. In essence, they are in the hands of the interpreters who are the only courtroom participants able to function in both languages (ASL and English). If the interpreters are not able to recognize errors, or they are making decisions to not correct the errors, it leaves the court at grave risk for inaccuracies in the testimony.

During the entering of direct evidence, there were significant errors made in the trials where simultaneous interpreting was used. Direct evidence is critical to a case, and Deaf witnesses want their "story" to be retold accurately by the interpreter. But, because they cannot hear, they have no access to the spoken language used by the lawyers, judge and interpreters. This means Deaf witnesses cannot monitor the accuracy of the interpretation. Instead, they have to rely on their faith in the interpreter's ability to comprehend their message and put it into spoken English in a way that successfully conveys the content, intent, register, affect and discourse goals. If Deaf people are to have access to the justice system, then obviously accurate interpreting is the foundation. The questions that need to be discussed by all courtroom stakeholders include: Does the

current predominant practice of using simultaneous interpreting allow for accurate interpretation to the degree that is
required in order for Deaf people's experiences to be heard
in a courtroom? Does the current model of interpreter education prepare interpreters to work in a consecutive mode of
interpretation? What degree of error is acceptable to the
Court?

During direct evidence, the interpreters split the
process, which meant that one interpreter handled all of the
ASL to spoken English utterances and the other dealt with
all the English to ASL utterances. In some trials the Deaf
witness was on the stand for over 40 minutes. With such an
arrangement, the interpreters were not able to spell themselves off every twenty minutes, which is current best practice. As with expert testimony, there were interpreting
errors made during direct evidence that were not corrected.
The error rate was far greater during the trials using simultaneous interpreting. It is difficult to know whether this
occurred because of interpreter fatigue or if the errors were
comprehension errors attributed to the early stages of interpretation cognitive processing models.

The expert witness testimony in this study possessed many of the features of legal language which make
it challenging to understand, and difficult to interpret accurately, such as technical terms, unusual prepositional phrases, and formality (Danet, 1980; O'Barr, 1982).
Unfortunately, as with any study of the product of interpretation, an assessment can only be offered about the accuracy of the work rather than the cognitive processes and deci-
sion-making steps used by the interpreter at the time of the
errors. The interpretation may have been more successful if
the interpreters had chosen to divide the testimony but not

split the process, thus compensating for the possibility of fatigue influencing their work. However, by splitting the process they were allowing themselves to focus on one target language consistently through the interpretation, as opposed to handling both target languages within the interaction.

The impact of the errors is that the Deaf witness was not able to relay the testimony with entire accuracy, which affects witness credibility and potential outcomes at a trial. Colin & Morris (1996) and Isham (1998) found that the "evaluation process" is the foundation of legal proceedings; everyone present assesses the degree to which other speakers are accurately, and credibly representing their actions, observations, and experience. When interpreters are used in the courtroom, they are one more element affecting the mutual evaluation of speakers. Further, when the interpretation is inaccurate then the whole evaluation process becomes problematic.

Discourse Events

An analysis of the trial data across the discourse events of expert witness testimony, the giving of direct evidence and cross-examination showed that there were substantially more errors made during expert witness testimony and direct evidence. This finding was true for both simultaneous and consecutive trials. There were far fewer errors made during cross-examination, which was expected, given the evidence being examined had already been entered in the direct evidence portion. The interpreters had already heard and seen the information being cross-examined. As well, the question and answer format gives a clearer focus for analyzing the information.

The results imply that the discourse frame and the courtroom event influence when interpreters may employ simultaneous or consecutive interpretation. There were times when the expert testimony work was effectively presented using simultaneous interpreting. This success appeared to occur when the testimony content was familiar to the interpreters, such as information about the Deaf community, the role of the interpreter and details about the interpreting process. However, there were also segments of the testimony which were complicated by linguistic terminology and numerous metaphors and similes. At these times, the interpretation was more successful when offered consecutively. The giving of expert testimony was conducted in a question and answer format, but the length of answers were often considerably longer and more technical or complicated than the answers given during direct evidence. This meant interpreters had to decide where to ask the witness to pause, and at times it also required the interpreters to use notes. It was observed that sometimes the interpreters waited too long before asking the witness to pause, and in doing so, some of the information was lost. This was likely due to the interpreter's memory capacity, and may also have been influenced by the fact that traditional basic interpreter education programs have not offered this training. When the interpreters used notes to record information they relied less on the strategy of asking the witness to repeat portions of an answer.

As reported in the interviews, the interpreters recognized that they needed better strategies to "chunk" messages consecutively, and that their notetaking practices did not support effective interpreting. While the interpreters reported using consecutive interpreting in their regular community work, it would appear that their experience with consecutive interpreting has been based on a method of "trial and error" as opposed to solid training.

The discourse frame also had an impact on the accuracy of the cross-examination event. Given the evidence was not new to the interpreters, the interpretation could be delivered successfully via simultaneous interpreting. The lawyers all preferred simultaneous interpreting to be used during cross-examination, in that it allowed for the natural cadence of quick question and response times, and for emotions to be more accurately conveyed. The goal of cross-examination is, as one lawyer described, "to put the witness off", and lawyers agreed the goal was realized more effectively when using simultaneous interpreting. When consecutive interpreting was used for cross-examination, the lawyers reported feeling dissatisfied with the interpretation. They agreed that it appeared to give the witness more time to compose their answers, and allowed them to relax more than when using simultaneous interpreting. One lawyer described the following:

> *I wanted to get the Deaf witness to admit to certain facts and appear confused. When the interpreters used simultaneous, I think I was more successful in presenting the inconsistencies in the witness's statements, and to also make them angry.*

Direct evidence, as a distinct discourse frame, benefited from the use of consecutive interpreting. The question and answer format lent itself to consecutive interpreting as the information was presented as a "natural" chunk of information. The question and answer dialogue also meant that the interpreters could very likely handle the amount of information without notetaking supports or the need for information to be repeated. While all Crown prosecutors agreed that they preferred simultaneous interpreting, when presented with the results of the study, one of the most experienced Crown prosecutors remarked:

> *What I want is convictions - so the interpreting has to be dead on. If taking it slower and using consecutive achieves that then I am for it. I just need to know the interpreters are doing the best they can to "get it right". It's what we have to do with the foreign language interpreters anyway. But it just takes longer...*

Bruton (1985) found that not all types of texts can be interpreted simultaneously, given the difficult conditions characterizing the materials. One of the conditions identified by Bruton was the lack of knowledge by the interpreter about the context, and that seems to have been a factor in examining the errors in some of the simultaneous interpretation of the expert and direct evidence events in these trials.

One of the opportunities that exists for interpreters is to examine the discourse frame within the interpreted event and learn to apply either simultaneous or consecutive interpreting strategies, depending on what is warranted. There has been a tendency within the field to view consecutive and simultaneous interpreting in dualistic terms. What seems more helpful, based on the results of this study, is to view them as strategies to facilitate interpreting and to recognize the need to use both within an interaction. In the context of legal settings, it would appear that expert witness tcstimony can be accomplished using both simultaneous and consecutive interpreting within a given testimony. However, given the error rate found when using simultaneous interpreting during direct evidence, the results suggest that interpreters would be wise to use consecutive interpreting for such a discourse event. Finally, cross-examination can be successfully managed by generally using simultaneous interpreting.

One of the aspects that was not addressed specifically in this study was how the different discourse styles interact in the courtroom. This study has revealed information about the components of language and how they are interpreted between language users, but there are many other interesting aspects of language use to be explored. For example, the discourse style of the judge and the lawyers is not always a shared form, nor is the witnesses' discourse style necessarily shared by the lawyers and judge. Given that language users create meaning based on their expectations or schemata, there are fascinating questions to consider about the schemata that Deaf people use in creating discourse when compared to the schemata of an English-speaking judge or lawyer. Investigations into this area would also be helpful to understanding how accurate interpretation can be provided in a legal environment.

Experiences of the Participants

The second research objective was to investigate the experiences of those involved in the courtroom interactions, by conducting interviews with interpreters, lawyers, judges and witnesses. The participants in the study were very knowledgeable concerning their "role" and offered informative material with regard to their experiences in these trials. Their openness and thoughtfulness concerning their perspectives on accurate interpretation and how best to accommodate Deaf people in legal proceedings was exceptional. It has given credence to the position that creating meaningful access to the courtroom for Deaf people who are utilizing ASL/English interpretation is best determined by including all stakeholders in the conversations about how best to provide service, as each perspective adds crucial information.

The following sections discuss some of the most cogent aspects of the interviews held with lawyers, judges, witnesses and interpreters.

Judges

For judges, the themes that emerged included the following: orientation to interpreting and deafness, understanding basic principles of ASL, positioning of interpreters, conferring, error correction, and witness control. Some of the judges had prior experience working with interpreters, while others had none. All judges commented on the need to create materials that would help courts understand the basic facts about ASL, including an orientation to matters of deafness and interpreting. The incidence of deafness is low, and a judge could go throughout his/her entire career without ever having a Deaf person involved in a court matter. The judges emphasized the type of information given by the expert witness was excellent in providing them with a context for the interpreting and some of the unique variables that need to be considered when working with Deaf people in the courtroom. One judge stressed how valuable the content of the expert witness testimony was to him:

> *If the case were serious and the trial going to be several weeks I would hope the Crown would employ a similar expert witness to set the stage. It really eliminated many of my questions and exposed me to information that I have never heard in my life. All judges should hear that witness.*

The judges indicated a need to feel the interpretation was accurate, and if the interpreters conferred with each other frequently, the judges questioned the reliability of the interpretation. The judges questioned if the legal system screens interpreters sufficiently for courtroom work, and two judges said they now had additional questions to ask of the interpreters before accepting them as courtroom interpreters. Judges expressed concern that errors made by interpreters were not consistently acknowledged and repaired clearly for the court. One of the helpful practices performed by one interpreting team was the use of the phrase "interpreter error...the correct information is....", so that they could tell when an error belonged to an interpreter versus when the change in answer was a witness choice.

There was a prevalent misunderstanding regarding attending behaviours required in ASL, whereby the interpreters nodded affirmatively while a Deaf witness was giving testimony. The behaviour is designed to give the Deaf person feedback that indicates the interpreters are understanding the witness, but the perception of non-signers is that this behaviour results in controlling or encouraging the witness and this is not an appropriate role for the interpreter. The judges further commented that the "attending behaviours" could be easily misconstrued as "encouraging the witness", and as such, the judge did not want interpreters to be "controlling the witness or events within the courtroom".

Lawyers

The lawyers expressed similar themes to the judges during the post-trial interviews, including the following: the importance of preparation, positioning so that interpreters and witnesses are visible at all times, the use of conferring between interpreters, strategies for managing error correction, conveying emotions, witness control and a preference for simultaneous interpreting over consecutive interpreting.

The lawyers were generally impressed with the skills and abilities of the interpreters, but some of the lawyers were concerned that the interpreters had neglected to ask important questions about the content of the trial. During the preparation conversations, some lawyers also identified that the specific linguistic or interpreting terminology used by the interpreter was unfamiliar to them, and as such, they had some difficulty grasping the significance of what the interpreter was attempting to tell them.

As with judges, lawyers felt it was critical that they see the interpreter at all times and also see the Deaf witness. This presents some challenges in terms of establishing sight lines necessary between Deaf witnesses and interpreters. This aspect of dealing with the uniqueness of a signing Deaf witness could be addressed in the preparation conversations, so that agreements are reached prior to the commencement of a trial.

Lawyers concurred with judges when asked to examine their perceptions of the interpreters conferring with one another. The theme in common for these participants is that they would prefer interpreters to ask permission prior to conferring with each other, and that they identify why it is necessary to do so. In the same light, the interviews conducted with lawyers and judges have indicated the ways in which error management must be addressed if the court is to have confidence in the interpretation. The difficulty in this area is the evidence that interpreters are not recognizing or correcting all the errors made, and lawyers and judges have no way of knowing when this is occurring in the trial.

The lawyers acknowledged they were also worried about the interpreters' ability to convey the emotional aspects of a given message from spoken English to ASL. The interpreters had not addressed this area with lawyers in their preparation conversation, and this may be an area that should be covered as one strategy to build confidence in the interpreting. The interpreters were able to successfully convey the affectual and emotional aspects throughout the trial; however, the lawyers said they based their fears on their misconception that ASL cannot convey emotions, and previous experiences with spoken language interpreters who were inconsistent in the delivery of emotional content.

Like judges, the lawyers also addressed witness control in their interviews. They questioned the strategies of interpreters to stop witnesses and ask them to repeat answers without first seeking the Court's direction.

Finally, all lawyers expressed a preference for simultaneous interpreting because of its apparent efficiency, but gave primary value to accuracy. The lawyers commented that consecutive interpreting seemed suitable for direct evidence but that they did not like it for cross-examination, given that it changed the cadence of such an examination. They also said that during expert witness testimony the consecutive interpreting seemed to truncate the information, which could have the potential impact of lessening the testimony.

Deaf Witnesses

Deaf witnesses had similar comments to the judges and lawyers when dealing with themes of interpreting, conferring, and error correction. There were some additional themes which emerged from the interviews with Deaf witnesses, and they included: courtroom protocol, interpreting behaviour, notetaking practices and their personal preferences when working with ASL/English interpreters.

The Deaf witnesses stressed the importance of the interpreter being confident in legal settings if they are going to interpret in them. The Deaf witnesses perceived the interpreters as competent and comfortable to work with if they produced ASL consistently, took the time necessary to indicate who was speaking prior to delivering the interpretation, and produced meaning-based interpreting. Ironically, in separate interviews, the Deaf witnesses agreed that the certified interpreter with the least amount of legal interpreting experience appeared to be the most confident and consistently produced messages that made visual sense in ASL. They also observed that this same interpreter had very few instances of stopping lawyers or witnesses to seek clarification. They trusted this interpreter's work and felt confident their narrative was understood.

Both Deaf witnesses preferred simultaneous interpreting, but they also commented on how much clearer the
interpreting was when the interpreters used consecutive
interpreting. Both witnesses suggested there is a need to
educate Deaf community members about simultaneous and
consecutive interpreting, given the dominant practice of
using simultaneous interpreting. As Deaf people have no
access to the spoken source language utterances, they are
not in a position to know when the interpreting is successful or not, and hence put their faith in the interpreter. The
evidence in this study is that there were many errors during
simultaneous interpreting and many of them occurred during direct evidence. One note of interest is that the Deaf
witnesses had a sense there were several errors in the
interpretation of expert witness testimony, but they assumed
the interpreters were handling their testimony more
successfully.

Like lawyers and judges, Deaf witnesses also
expressed concern about the conferring behaviour of the
interpreters. It is possible that the interpreters conferred
more frequently in these trials given they knew they were
participating in a study of interpreting accuracy. However,
it seems the times during the trials where the interpreters
conferred were when the question was ill-formed, or the
witness's answer was detail-laden. The common theme that
links the experiences of judges, lawyers and Deaf witnesses is the concern for how frequently this occurs and how little control the Court seems to have over it.

The witnesses identified a strategy that worked well
in the courtroom that surrounded error correction. They
noted the interpreter who was interpreting from ASL to

spoken English would correct an answer, and the other interpreter would sign in ASL what the interpreter had said. This practice allowed the Deaf witness to confirm the accuracy of the answer, and allowed the Deaf witness to feel a more "equal participant" in the proceedings. It also contributed to increased trust in the interpreting.

The Deaf witnesses stressed they were affected by the lack of professionalism within the interpreting team who worked Trial Three. They could see the interpreting quality deteriorate after twenty minutes and questioned the interpreter's decision not to switch. The Deaf witnesses commented that the dynamics between the team - frustration, anger, signed communication between the two interpreters - was annoying to them, and caused them to feel anxious about how the interpreters would handle their upcoming testimony. It is clear that interpreters' behaviour is closely watched by Deaf witnesses and as such, affects the witnesses' experience in the courtroom.

Expert Witness

The expert witness commented on many of the same areas as the judges, lawyers and Deaf witnesses. What was significant in the interview with the expert witness was the need for interpreters to explore preparation conversations from the perspective of the witness, in addition to their own interpreter perspectives. One out of four interpreting teams approached the expert by exploring her goals and what message she thought was critical to leave with the Court. This strategy was more effective than solely telling the witness how they could support the interpreters in completing their work. The expert witness submitted a document to the

Court, and in retrospect, she realized that none of the interpreters had thought to ask about this area. Had the interpreters been able to read the document in advance, there may have been far fewer errors made during expert witness testimony.

The expert witness has many years of experience using consecutive and simultaneous interpreting, and based on that experience, she noted some of the interpreters appeared unsure of when and how to stop a speaker, and how to manage the consecutive process to produce smooth transitions between speakers or signers and interpreters. She noted that in her experience interpreters have not had training in consecutive interpreting as a foundation for simultaneous interpreting, and this can affect how effectively it is used in the community.

Positioning was also an issue for the expert witness who had the experience of interpreters standing in front of her while she was addressing the judge. It seems clear that positioning needs to be negotiated and planned in advance in order to reduce the intrusiveness of some placements.

Lastly, the expert witness also raised the issue of notetaking strategies, commenting that one team was unprepared for the potential need for notes, and had to stop the court proceedings during her testimony to get the materials. The expert witness questioned the decision making approaches of the team, stressing this would have been the perfect time for the interpreters to switch positions as opposed to using notes. The witness also wondered about the notetaking protocols used, stressing the time to write notes appeared to be very time consuming and did not result in a consistently accurate interpretation.

Interpreters

The themes that arose from interviews with interpreters included: preparation topics and strategies, interpreting, dealing with courtroom discourse, notetaking practices, and team processes.

Overall, the interpreters recognized that the quality of their interpreting was better when they used consecutive interpreting, but consistently they said that they needed to have more practice with consecutive interpreting in order to have the process go more smoothly for all participants. The interpreters also identified how they need to employ more consecutive interpreting into their regular work. One interpreter spoke of their increased awareness of how much more accurate their interpreting could be when using consecutive interpreting based on the experience of offering consecutive interpreting on the first day, and then providing simultaneous interpreting on the second day. This same interpreter, during the simultaneous interpreting trial, reverted to consecutive interpreting for a section of it, and also utilized a very long processing time for some ASL to English answers. When asked about these decisions, the interpreter commented:

> *I just knew I didn't have enough information. The judge was speaking very slowly, and I wasn't clear on their point. I needed to hear the whole comparison between taking an oath and affirming before I could make it make sense in ASL. As for using a longer processing time, I was thinking the ASL answer was quite complicated, so I knew I needed to understand it first, before I could make the court understand it.*

There were times when the volume of information and pace of the courtroom proceedings affected all of the interpreters, who spoke to the need to just "keep up". Such is the pressure that exists in courtrooms for interpreters, and yet producing target language constructions without processing the meaning creates a scenario where Deaf witnesses cannot effectively participate in the trial.

The interpreters identified what worked well for them as teams. They commented that an effective team was built on a foundation of trusting the other person's interpreting skills, and seeing the team as responsible for the accuracy of the work, as opposed to having the individual interpreter held accountable for the error. In Trial Three, the team struggled with team processes which affected the accuracy of the interpreting. They were able to identify what did not work well for them, and how they should have handled the situation differently. The concept that interpreters can continue to work a sixty minute block of interpretation, without a break, and still produce grammatically correct and content accurate information must be challenged. The evidence suggests that when cognitive fatigue starts to impact the interpreter, regardless of strategies such as notetaking, the interpreting work is still negatively affected. This may also speak to an additional area of training needed by interpreters, so that effective team work strategies are part of the skill set of interpreters working in legal settings.

Preparation Strategies

The third objective of the study was to investigate

the preparation strategies of interpreters working together as a team, when preparing lawyers about the task of working with interpreters and when preparing with witnesses.

The interpreters engaged in preparation conversations, and a series of common topic areas were found among the teams. These common topics included the following:

- How best to share the assignment;
- How to support and cue the working interpreter;
- Offering cues in ASL or English;
- Preparation topics with witnesses and lawyers; and
- Ways in which the Court can support accurate interpretation.

Upon reflection, the interpreters identified that they should have been more diligent in gaining preparation information from the expert witness and content specific details from the Crown prosecutor. If they had information in advance, it may have resulted in fewer errors being made during expert testimony, as well as during direct evidence. One team realized that even the most basic details would have been helpful, for example, the team knew the charge was sexual assault, but they neglected to ask where the alleged assault took place. In the actual trial, the interpreters had to ask the Crown to repeat the name of the town, but had they asked for this information prior to the commencement of the trial, there would have been no reason for the interruption.

Despite engaging in preparation strategies with each other, there were some additional topic areas that could have been helpful for the interpreters to canvass with each

other. These additional topic areas included:
- Dealing with frozen text such as oaths;
- Specific lexical choices needed for the trials;
- Case details available from lawyers;
- Notetaking strategies;
- Witness reassurances about note disposal after trials; and
- Preparation with expert witnesses focused on goals and content.

Information obtained in the interviews with lawyers suggests that interpreters presented information about the role and functioning of the interpreters that was too detailed, and therefore less helpful to the lawyers. The lawyers also suggested the need for interpreters to secure more case-specific details when preparing for trials.

The Deaf witness who participated in Trial Three, in which the interpreter took many notes during expert testimony, disliked the notetaking practice. It took far too long and it was questionable whether the interpreting was more accurate because of it. Both Deaf witnesses identified that the interpreters did not prepare them for the fact that they may need to take notes, nor how those notes would be disposed of, both of which could have been addressed.

Cognitive Processes

The final objective of the study was to explore two aspects of the cognitive processes of interpreting (source language comprehension and target language comprehension) by examining the notes taken by interpreters and used as interpreting tools while interpreting a trial. Two aspects of cognitive processes are presented here that address the use of notes in the courtroom, and the target language/error rates.

Notetaking Practices

All interpreter participants acknowledged they rarely used notetaking strategies and as such, were unsure how to use notes in a way that supports the delivery of accurate interpreting. One interpreting team chose to record the proper spelling of witnesses' names, make note of dates in question and draft spatial maps based on witnesses' descriptions. This type of information appeared useful in this context.

One interpreter in this study used notes during a trial employing consecutive interpreting. The notes revealed the interpreter had written verbatim what was offered in the witness's answer or lawyer's question. This did not support accurate interpretation, in that the adherence to written English then meant the interpreter still had to apply a cognitive model of interpreting to the message in order to process it for meaning. This greatly increased the time span between writing down the information and presenting it in ASL. In those programs where consecutive interpreting is taught prior to simultaneous interpreting, strategies such as using a discourse map or symbols that allow for the interpreter to process the message as they are hearing it, record the ideas, not the words in the original grammar and then produce the message based on the map, are taught (Winston, 1998). These sophisticated tools may have enhanced the interpretation if used in this setting.

Target Language and Error Rate

There were significantly more interpreting errors when the interpreters were working into American Sign Language, which is also not surprising given the fact that ASL is the second language of the majority of the interpreters in this study. Seleskovitch (1998) found that interpreters who work into their first language, sometimes known as their "A" language, present more successful interpretation than when they work into their "B" language, or second language. That same finding appears to be supported in this study. In this same light, the results of this study may indicate the need for increased use of Deaf interpreters in courtrooms. When there are teams of Deaf and non-deaf interpreters placed in the courtroom, the Deaf interpreter is in fact working into their "A" or "first" language. Further study of the use of Deaf interpreters would be useful in this context.

There were several types of errors that emerged, and they included: ASL grammatical errors, semantic errors in ASL, source language intrusions from English found in the ASL, omissions of content, additions that were not found in the source message, and linking ideas in ways not found in the original message. Some of these errors were likely caused by difficulties with source language comprehension, which is one of the earliest stages of most of the cognitive models of interpretation. Other error patterns seem to indicate the interpreters understood the source message but lacked sufficient target language grammatical knowledge in order to offer an equivalent message. This resulted in source language intrusions in both ASL and spoken English.

Interpreting Model

The study was an opportunity to review the cognitive processes that interpreters use in their work. The following figure provides a model that summarizes the steps utilized by interpreters when producing meaning-based interpretation, and offers a blend of some of the cognitive models reviewed in Chapter Two. The model brings together the role of context, linguistic and cultural schema and the decision making process that involves choosing consecutive or simultaneous interpreting. Figure 5.1 is followed by an explanation of the sub-steps of each stage.

Figure 5.1
Steps of a Meaning-Based Interpreting Model

CONTEXTUAL FACTORS

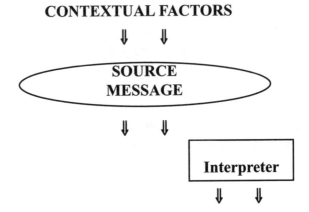

Assess Contextual   ⇒ 1. Comprehend Source Message
Factors

                       2. Apply Contextual & Linguistic
                          Schema

                          3. Formulate Equivalent Message

Monitor Interpreting ⇒ 4. Produce Target Process
Process   Language Interpretation

Figure 5.2
Steps of a Meaning-Based Interpreting Model

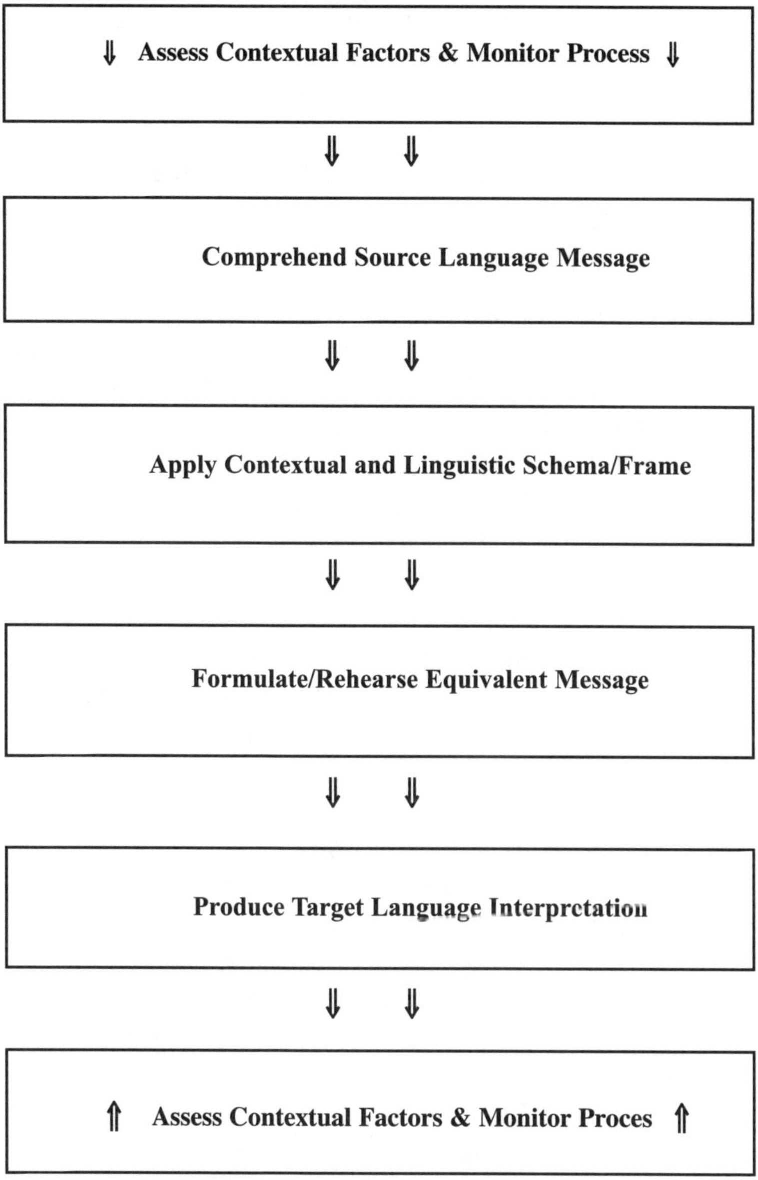

⇩ **Assess Contextual Factors & Monitor Process** ⇩

⇩   ⇩

Comprehend Source Language Message

⇩   ⇩

Apply Contextual and Linguistic Schema/Frame

⇩   ⇩

Formulate/Rehearse Equivalent Message

⇩   ⇩

Produce Target Language Interpretation

⇩   ⇩

⇧ **Assess Contextual Factors & Monitor Proces** ⇧

Explanation of the Model

Providing interpreting services occurs within a context of receiving a source message, and then assessing the context as it impacts upon the message.

The message must be analyzed for its components of meaning, and then equivalents found in the target language. Interpreters must constantly monitor their assessment of the context and production of the message.

1. Assess Contextual Factors & Monitor Process

Throughout the interpreted interaction, the interpreter is constantly assessing contextual factors and their impact upon communication. This includes assessing such factors as:

- The relationship between the parties in the interaction;
- Formal and informal power structures represented;
- Similarities/differences in background/ experience of parties involved; and
- Emotional overlay of interaction.

2. Monitor Process

Throughout the interpreted interaction, the interpreter monitors the communication process. This includes such factors as:

- Verifying comprehension and seeking clarification when needed/appropriate;
- Slowing the process to allow for movement between simultaneous and consecutive forms of interpreting as determined appropriate;

- Checking for and correcting errors as appropriate; and
- Verifying comprehension of consumers.

3. Comprehend Source Language Message

In order for this stage to occur, the interpreter must possess bilingual and bicultural knowledge and skills, and honed text analysis skills, to support the comprehension of the original message. The interpreter draws upon his/her:

- Syntactic knowledge;
- Semantic knowledge;
- Associated knowledge/background experience;
- Cultural awareness; and
- Contextual knowledge.

The interpreter is required to process information at lexical, phrase, sentential and discourse levels in order to identify deep-structure meaning, and to recognize the frame that must be applied in order to realize the goals of the speaker/signer.

4. Apply Contextual and Linguistic Schema/Frame

This stage involves the application of the interpreter's on-going assessment of the contextual factors influencing the interaction, such as cross-cultural and cross-linguistic awareness, linguistic competence, and the experiential/cultural frame of the parties.

The interpreter must determine whether to use consecutive or simultaneous interpreting for the message, in order to maintain equivalence and;

support genuine communication access to all
participants.

5. Formulate/Rehearse Equivalent Message
After processing the information at lexical,
phrase, sentential and discourse levels in order to
identify deep-structure meaning, and to recognize
the frame that must be applied in order to realize the
goals of the speaker/signer, the interpreter is prepared for this stage.

The interpreter makes cultural and linguistic
choices - planning, formulating and reviewing elements to be used in expressing an equivalent message in the target language. In legal contexts, more
time will be spent at this stage when dealing with
complex texts, consumers using non-standard linguistic forms, or when the interpreter is a relatively
inexperienced interpreter.

6. Produce Target Language Interpretation
The interpreter formulates the Target
Language message based on the previous stages,
while drawing on his/her knowledge of:
- Syntactic knowledge;
- Semantic knowledge;
- Associated knowledge/background
  experience;
- Cultural awareness; and
- Contextual knowledge.
This stage is influenced by physical, psycho-
logical, and cross-language modality factors such
as fatigue, personal reaction of the content of the

message, and dual-tasking requirements of making the transition into a second language and a second language modality. Making the transition between two language forms is unique to sign language interpreters.

Other Findings

Interpreter Utterances

In each of the trials, there was evidence of interpreters creating utterances. This finding is consistent with the findings of research on ASL/English interpreters working in medical settings (Metzger, 1999). What is somewhat surprising, though, is that not all interpreter generated utterances were fully interpreted so that the participants could understand what the interpreters have said or signed. If interpreters are to be perceived as neutral, and as vehicles for making all utterances accessible to all parties in the courtroom, then this behaviour is inconsistent with that goal. One of the best practices that was evident in one trial is described as follows: If Interpreter A created an interpreter generated utterance, for example, asking a lawyer to repeat the question, Interpreter B would sign that information for the benefit of the Deaf witness.

When utterances were frequently not interpreted for the Court they were often of the form of signed utterances between interpreters, for example, interpreters signaling each other that it was time to switch positions. These signed utterances were clear to the Deaf witness, but the judge and lawyers present in the courtroom had no idea what the interpreters were saying. This caused one judge to offer the following comment:

> *I need to control what happens in the courtroom.*
> *While I understand the interpreters will need to spell*
> *each other off and sometimes confer with each other,*
> *they should not be having other communication*
> *between them that is not audible to me.*

Contributions of the Study

The study was designed to respond to limitations outlined with the literature. These limitations were outlined as follows:

1. An apparent lack of research examining simultaneous and consecutive interpreting in legal settings;

2. Studies of spoken language interpreting and cognitive processing models present strong arguments in favour of consecutive interpreting producing more accurate interpretation, however there is a prevalent practice among sign language interpreters to use simultaneous interpreting in courtrooms;

3. A tendency for interpreters to stress the importance of preparation with those involved in a trial process, however there appear to be no studies that have defined the scope of preparation completed by interpreters;

4. An apparent lack of information to be gained from notes taken during interpreting about the comprehension of the source message and reconstruction into the target language;

5. A lack of research that included the experiences of

all courtroom participants who rely on interpretation, namely, judges, lawyers, Deaf witnesses and expert witnesses.

The following section outlines how this research addresses these five limitations.

This study is one of the first to explore the use of consecutive and simultaneous interpreting with interpreters who use ASL and English as the language pairs within a legal context. While there is research that supports consecutive interpreting as a more accurate approach to interpreting, all of that research was conducted with spoken language interpreters and was not specific to legal arenas. The results of this study suggest support for the use of consecutive interpreting in legal assignments.

Secondly, this research was conducted specifically with sign language interpreters and showed statistically significant differences between the accuracy of consecutive interpreting when compared to simultaneous interpreting. It also demonstrated how discourse events, such as expert witness testimony, the entering of direct evidence, and cross-examination can influence the production of accurate interpretation.

Thirdly, the data underscore the importance of preparation work as a necessary step for supporting accurate interpretation, and how interpreters can broaden the scope of preparation to enhance their readiness to perform their task. As well, when preparing with lawyers, Deaf witnesses and expert witnesses, interpreters would be well-advised to examine the language analogies used to describe their work, and to also inquire about the goals of the witnesses in giving testimony.

Fourthly, because notes are one strategy that can be used while providing consecutive interpreting, this study exposed a practice that does not support accurate interpreting. Namely, the direct verbatim recording of source language messages does not contribute to effective consecutive interpreting. There is a need for interpreters to listen to the source message, and decode it prior to recording the ideas and concepts in a discourse map, in order to effectively use time and to reduce source language intrusions. In some current interpreter education programs, these skills are learned when consecutive interpreting is taught as a foundation to successful simultaneous interpreting. Bruton (1985) and Lambert (1989) emphasized that it is through a progression of exercises aimed at teaching the interpreter to grasp, analyze, remember and then reproduce the message of the speaker that interpreters can eventually proceed to acceptable simultaneous interpretation where required or desired, and it would appear the results of this study support such processes.

Fifthly, the experiences of those relying on interpretation, including Deaf people and agents of the court, were documented in this study. Their perspectives inform this study and offer further insight into the application of simultaneous and consecutive interpreting in the courtroom.

The study was a comparative analysis of simultaneous interpreting and consecutive interpreting across three discourse events. The theoretical rationale for this study was derived from the research on cognitive processing and interpreting, including the work of Cokely, Seleskovitch, and Berk-Seligson. The results indicate that consecutive interpreting produced more accurate interpretation as compared to simultaneous interpreting. This finding is consistent with the theories of cognitive processing and also with the previous research of Alexieva (1991), Bruton (1985), and Mikkelson (1995) that reported consecutive interpreting results in great accuracy in the transmission of the message. The findings of this research also support the previous findings of Cokely (1992), who found that the number of interpreting errors decrease with greater processing time. The results also imply that discourse events can influence when simultaneous interpreting can be successfully used, for example some segments of expert witness testimony and for cross-examination. Consecutive interpreting was more successful for complicated parts of expert testimony and for the entering of direct evidence. The need for preparation between interpreters, as well as between interpreters and lawyers, interpreters and Deaf witnesses, and interpreters and expert witnesses was highlighted in this study.

Implications

The results concerning consecutive interpreting and simultaneous interpreting may encourage interpreters and interpreter educators to be cognizant of the practices that contribute to accurate interpreting, especially in legal contexts. The findings contribute to a better understanding of the kinds of errors made when using simultaneous interpreting, and how errors are missed even when working in teams where the interpreters are attempting to monitor each other's work. As well, the findings suggest that interpreters need to use more effective preparation and notetaking strategies as a tool to support consecutive interpreting.

The results may be important for interpreter

educators who are lobbying for consecutive interpreting courses as an integral part of the curriculum. The results also suggest that interpreters could benefit from being able to identify the discourse frames that are most effectively interpreted using consecutive and simultaneous strategies. There appears to be a need for all interpreter practitioners, not just those taking current interpreter education programs, to benefit from solid training in the use of consecutive interpreting strategies and notetaking practices. If interpreters are to provide the most accurate interpreting possible in legal contexts, then the current practice of providing service using simultaneous interpreting must be challenged.

The experiences of Deaf people need to be considered when making decisions that will either provide meaningful access to the language of the courtroom, or will provide the appearance of access. The use of simultaneous interpreting, gives the appearance of access, but in this research it produced a higher degree of errors, when contrasted to consecutive interpreting. Other agents of the court have no ability to assess the accuracy of interpreting, and hence are dependent on interpreters to acknowledge errors and to take the steps needed to prevent or reduce errors.

The perspectives of lawyers must also be taken into account when interpreters are negotiating the interpreting services to be provided in the courtroom. It is clear from the study that lawyers do not favour the use of consecutive interpreting during the cross-examination process. However, there is agreement from all agents of the court that the interpretation must be as accurate as possible, and if that means using consecutive interpreting for segments or all of the trial, then that must be negotiated.

There are many opportunities to educate lawyers and judges about the work of sign language interpreters, the interpreting process and features that arise when working with Deaf people in the courtroom. This study suggests that these professionals are very interested in the work of interpreters and lack information that would help them in their respective roles. Having an understanding of what interpreters do in the courtroom should prove to be effective in enhancing the trial experience for Deaf people as well ensuring an accurate record is entered.

Finally, this research broadens the domain of what is understood about consecutive and simultaneous interpreting when used by interpreters who are working between languages that differ in modality, namely a signed language and a spoken language. The research has now been broadened to include the previously unrecognized samples of ASL/English interpreters in legal contexts.

Recommendations

The study makes the following recommendations on the basis of its findings and a review of the literature. Suggestions include the following:

1. Educational programs be developed for ASL /English interpreters working in legal settings to expand their knowledge and use of consecutive and simultaneous interpreting, legal discourse and protocol, notetaking strategies, and effective team processes which include preparation guidelines. This training should also include how to present the need for simultaneous and consecutive interpreting

when communicating with agents of the court and with Deaf witnesses.

2. Orientation materials be designed to educate agents of the court, such as judges and lawyers, about the intricacies of working with sign language interpreters and Deaf witnesses. Opportunities to collaborate with Deaf community representatives exist to present cross-cultural training for the legal community.

3. Sign language interpreter education programs incorporate training in consecutive interpreting as a foundation for accurate simultaneous interpreting, and as a necessary skill set for their professional practice which will require using both consecutive and simultaneous interpreting.

4. Additional research be conducted in order to understand the use of consecutive and simultaneous interpreting in contexts other than legal settings, for example medical and mental health contexts, with both sign language interpreters and spoken language interpreters.

5. Additional research be conducted into the use of Deaf interpreters in courtrooms and how their presence and mastery of ASL and Deaf culture may contribute to accurate interpretation.

The next step is to integrate the results of the present research into legal contexts, and the interpreter education setting. It is important that interpreters, Deaf people, and agents of the court develop a better understanding and acceptance of strategies that contribute to effective and accurate interpreting in legal settings. With a better understanding, and more thorough approaches to educating those who work in legal contexts there comes an opportunity for consistent, accurate interpreting. An important step in improving service delivery for Deaf and non-deaf people requires educating the next generation of interpreters so that the current practice of providing simultaneous interpreting does not remain the dominant practice.

Limitations of the Study

The following limitations in the research methods must be acknowledged. The first pertains to the researcher. Being a professional interpreter and an interpreter educator, my identification with the profession may have influenced my analysis and led me to overemphasize the importance of some segments of the research findings. An attempt to minimize this limitation was made by inviting peer analysts and linguistic experts to comment on the preliminary findings. By using this process, it was hoped that any professional biases of the researcher could be detected and rectified.

Another potential limitation of the study arises from the preparation for the mock trial stage of the research. The interpreters who participated indicated a knowledge of consecutive interpreting and hence had their own notctaking strategics. The information I offered to them could have been more structured which may have resulted in more useful data to emerge from the notes.

As well, the mock trials had an element of artificiality to them, in that the Deaf witnesses were playing a role, which may have impacted on the emotional aspects which often emerge in a trial. However, in interviews with the witnesses after the trials, both Deaf witnesses indicated that they felt angry at points with some of the lawyers' questioning techniques, which seems to indicate that they took the role seriously and were able to react emotionally to the context of the mock trial.

Lastly, the approach of using four mock trials limits the generalizability of the findings, but does provide rich information about the accuracy of the two approaches of interpretation in the legal context. Also, by definition, the lawyers and judges who participated in this study may have been more sensitive and tolerant towards working with interpreters and Deaf witnesses, and hence may not represent the majority of lawyers and judges.

Conclusion

The study has provided descriptions of the differences in interpreting accuracy between consecutive and simultaneous interpreting. It has also provided information and reasons for the interpreting accuracy and interpreting errors found in the trials. Through this study some questions have been answered, and many require further investigation.

The goal of any interpreter is to provide the most accurate interpretation possible in any interpreted interaction. In legal contexts, the consequences of interpreting errors are grave. The dominant practice in ASL/English courtroom interpreting has been examined and challenged in this study. If interpreters want to provide the best quality of service possible then it will require some changes to the dominant practice of providing simultaneous interpreting. Such a change requires interpreters, as well as Deaf people and agents of the court, to reconsider the assumptions underlying their practices, and to be willing to embrace new strategies.

REFERENCES

Adams, B. (1997). Using consecutive interpreting. **The Well-Being Gazette.** Autumn, 5-6.

Alexieva, B. (1991). **The optimum text in simultaneous interpreting: a cognitive approach to interpreters' training.** Paper presented at the Annual meetings of the First Language International Conference (Elsinore, Denmark, May 31-June 02, 1991).

Allioni, S. (1989). Towards a grammar of consecutive interpretation. In L. Gran & J. Dodds (Eds.), **The theoretical and practical aspects of teaching conference interpretation.** (pp. 191-197). Udine, Italia: Companotto Editore.

Anderson, L. (1994). Simultaneous interpretation: Contextual and translation aspects. In S. Lambert & B. Moser-Mercer (Eds.), **Bridging the gap: Empirical studies in simultaneous interpretation.** (pp. 101-102). Philadelphia: John Benjamins.

AVLIC (1996). **Interpreting in Legal Settings: An AVLIC Position Paper.** Edmonton: AVLIC Publications.

Baker, A. (1995). Conflicts between the ethical confidentiality requirement and legal obligations to disclose. In **A confluence of diverse relationships: Proceedings of the Thirteenth National Convention of the Registry of Interpreters for the Deaf.** (pp. 21-39). Silver Spring, MD: Registry of Interpreters for the Deaf.

Baker, C. & Cokely, D. (1980). **American Sign Language: A teacher's resource text on grammar and culture.** Washington,D.C., Gallaudet University Press.

Barnwell, D. (1989). **Court interpretation: A need for a certification process.** Paper presented at the Annual meeting of the Southeast Conference on Languages and Literature. (Orlando, FL., Feb. 24, 1989).

Benmaman, V. (1992). Terminological impact of different legal systems on court interpreting. In M. Valiquette (Ed.), **Translating in North America - A community of interest. Proceedings of the Third Congress of the CIT Regional Center for North America.** (pp. 214-222). Ottawa, On: Canadian Translators and Interpreters Council.

Benmaman, V. (1996). The use of cognates in the courtroom. In M.M. Jerome-O'Keeffe (Ed.), **Global vision: Proceedings of the 37th Annual Conference of the American translators Association.** (pp. 133-139). Alexandria, VA: American Translators Association.

Berk-Seligson, S. (1990). **The bilingual courtroom.** Chicago: University of Chicago Press.

Brown, G. & G. Yule. (1996). **Discourse analysis.** *Cambridge*: Cambridge University Press.

Bruton, K. (1985). Consecutive interpreting - the theoretical approach. In Thomas, N. (Ed.), **Interpreting as a language teaching technique - Proceedings of a conference.** University of Salford, England. Centre for Information Language Teaching and Research.

Cambell, D.& J. Stanley. (1963). Experimental and Quasi- Experimental Designs for Reserach. Rand McNally: Chicago.

Carr, S., Roberts, R., Dufour, A., & Steyn, D. (Eds.) (1995). **The Critical Link: Interpreters in the Community.** Philadelphia, PA: John Benjamins North America.

Chernov,G. (1992). Message redundancy and message anticipation in simultaneous interpretation. In S. Lambert & B. Moser-Mercer (Eds.), **Bridging the gap: Emperical research in simultaneous interpretation.** (pp. 139-153). Philadelphia: John Benjamins.

Cokely, D. (1992). **Interpretation: A sociolinguistic model.** Burtonsville, MD: Linstok Press.

Cokely, D. (Ed.) (1992). **Sign language interpreters and interpreting.** Burtonsville, MD: Linstok Press.

Colin, J. & Morris, R. (1996). **Interpreters and the Legal Process.** Winchester; Waterside Press.

Colonomos, B. (1992). **Interpreting Process: A working model.** Unpublished papers.

Conley, J., & W. O'Barr. (1990). **Rules Versus Relationships: The Ethnography of Legal Discourse.** Chicago: University of Chicago Press.

Daro, V. (1990). Speaking speed during simultaneous interpretation: A discussion of its neuropsychological aspects and possible contributions to teaching. In L. Gran & C. Taylor (Eds.), **Aspects of applied and experimental research on conference interpretation.** (pp. 83-92). Udine, Italia: Campanotta Editore.

Daro, V. (1994). Non-linguistic factors influencing simultaneous interpretation. In S. Lambert & B. Moser-Mercer (Eds.), **Bridging the gap: Emperical research in simultaneous interpretation.** (pp. 249-271). Philadelphia: John Benjamins.

Daro, V. (1995). Attentional, auditory, and memory indexes as prerequisites for simultaneous interpreting. In J. Tommola (Ed.), **Topics in interpreting research.** (pp. 3-10). Turku, Finland: University of Turku.

Daro, V., & Fabbro, F. (1994). Verbal memory during simultaneous interpreting: Effects of phonological interference. **Applied Linguistics,** 15, 365-381.

Dejongh, E.M. (1992). **An Introduction to Court Interpreting: Theory, and Practice.** Lanham, MD: University Press of America.

Dillinger, M. (1994). Comprehension during interpreting. In Lambert, S., & B. Moser-Mercer. (Eds.), **Bridging the Gap: Emperical research in simultaneous interpretation.** Philadelphia, PA: John Benjamins North America.

Downing, B. & Tillery, K. (1992). **Professional training for community interpreters: A report on models of interpreting training and the value of training.** Minneapolis, MN: Minnesota University.

Egnatovitch, R. (1996). Old school of thought; deaf interpreter. Views, 13, 7, 22.

Eldridge v. British Colombia. **Supreme Court of Canada Decision,** Oct. 09, 1997. File 24896.

Engberg-Pedersen,E. (1995). Point of view expressed through shifters. In K. Emmorey & J. Reilly (Eds.), **Language, Gesture and Space.** (pp. 133-155). Hillsdale, NJ: Lawrence Erlbaum Associates.

Gibbons, J. (1990). Applied Linguistics in Court. **Applied Linguistics,** 11, 229-237.

Gibbons, J. (1996). Distortions in the Police interview revealed by videotape. **Applied Linguistics,** 3, 2, 289-298.

Gile, D. (1991). The processing capacity in conference interpretation. **Babel: International Journal of Translation,** 3, 1, 15-27.

Gile, D. (1995). Fidelity assessment in consecutive interpretation: An experiment. **Target: International Journal of Translation**, 7, 1, 151-164.

Gilmore, D. (1992). Fair hearings for the language-handicapped; The need for competence in court interpreting. In M. Valiquette (Ed.), **Translating in North America - A community of interest. Proceedings of the Third Congress of the CIT Regional Center for North America.** (pp. 223-233). Ottawa, Ontario: Canadian Translators and Interpreters Council.

Glasser, B. & Straus,A. (1967). Discovery of substantive theory. In W. Filstead (Ed.), **Qualitative methodology.** (pp. 228-297). Chicago, IL: Rand McNally.

Gonzalex, R.D., Vasquez, V.F., & H. Mikkelson. (1991). **Fundamentals of Court Interpretation: Theory, Policy and Practice.** Durham, NC: Carolina Academic Press.

Hill, J. (1978). Consecutive interpreting in advanced language work. **META**, 24, 4, 442-450.

Hulston, J. (1990). A comparison between information-processing and the analysis/control approaches to language learning. **Applied Linguistics**, 11, 1,30-44.

Humphrey, J. (1997). Chopping down and reconstructing a tree. **META**, 42, 3, 515-521.

Humphrey, J. & Alcorn, B. (1995). **So you want to be an interpreter? An introduction to sign language interpreting.** Amarillo, TX: HMB Publishers.

Humphrey, J., & D. Russell. (1994). **Interpreting in Legal Settings; An AVLIC Position Paper.** Edmonton, AB: AVLIC Publications.

Isham, W. (1993). Memory for form after simulta-neous interpretation: Comparisons of Language, modality, and process. In M.L. McIntire (Ed.), **Interpreting: The art of cross-cultural mediation: Proceedings of the Ninth National Convention of the Registry of Interpreters for the Deaf.** (pp. 60-69). Silver Spring, MD: Registry of Interpreters for the Deaf.

Isham, W. (1994). Memory for form after simultane-ous interpretation: Evidence both for and against deverbal-ization. In S. Lambert & B. Moser-Mercer (Eds.), **Bridging the gap: Emperical research in simultaneous interpreta-tion.** (pp. 191-211). Philadelphia: John Benjamins.

Isham, W. (1995). On the relevance of signed lan-guages to research in interpretation. **Target: International Journal of Translation,** 7, 1, 135-149.

Isham, W., & Lane, H. (1993). Simultaneous inter-pretation and the recall of source-language sentences. **Language and Cognitive Processes,** 8, 3, 241-264.

Isham, W., & Lane, H. (1994). A common concep-tual code in bilinguals: Evidence from simultaneous inter-pretation. **Sign Language Studies,** 85, 291-316.

Janzen, T., (1997). Pragmatic and syntactic features of topics in American Sign Language. **META,** 42, 3, 502-515.

Komesaroff, L. (1998). **The politics of language practices in deaf education.** Unpublished doctoral disser-tation. Deakin University, Faculty of Education, Melbourne, Australia.

Lambert, S. (1984). An introduction to consecutive interpretation. In M.L. McIntire (Ed.), **New dialogues in interpreter education: Proceedings of the Fourt National Conference of Interpreter Trainers Convention.** (pp. 76-98). Silver Spring, MD: RID Publications.

Lambert, S. (1991). Aptitude testing for simultaneous interpretation at the University of Ottawa. **META**, 36, I4, 586-594.

Lambert, S., & B. Moser-Mercer. (Eds.) (1994). **Bridging the Gap: Emperical research in simultaneous interpretation.** Philadelphia, PA: John Benjamins North America.

Lang, M. (1991). **Discourse analysis and the translator.** Unpublished paper.

Larson, M. (1984). **Meaning-Based translation: A guide to cross-language equivalency.** Lanham, MD: University Press of America.

Laster, K., and Taylor, V. (1994). **Interpreters and the Legal System.** Leichhardt, NSW: The Federation Press.

Livingston,S., Singer, B., & Abrahamson, T. (1994). Effectiveness compared: ASL interpretation vs. transliteration. **Sign Language Studies**, 82, 1-53.

Kohn, K., & Kalina, S. (1996). The strategic dimension of interpreting. **META**, 4 , 1, 118-138.

Klima, E. & Bellugi, U. (1979). **The signs of language.** Cambridge, MA: Harvard University Press.

Macken, E., Perry, K, & Haas, C. (1995). American Sign Language & heterogeneous communication systems. **Sign Language Studies**, 89, 363-413.

Mallery-Ruganis, D., & Fischer, S. (1991). Characteristics that contribute to effective simultaneous communication. **American Annals of the Deaf,** 136, 5, 401-408.

Mayberry, R. (1995). Mental phonology and language comprehension, or what does that sign mistake mean? In K. Emmorey & J. Reilly (Eds.), **Language, Gesture and Space.** (pp. 333-335). Hillsdale, NJ: Lawrence Erlbaum Associates.

Metzger, M. (1995). **The paradox of neutrality: A comparison of interpreters' goals with the reality of interactive discourse.** Unpublished dissertation, Georgetown University, Washington, D.C.

Mikkelson, H. (1992). **The Interpreter's Edge.** Spreckels, CA: Acebo Press.

Mikkelson, H. (1996). **Towards a Redefinition of the Role of Court Interpreters.** Unpublished papers (Internet)

Mikkelson, H. (1996). The professionalization of community interpreting. In M.M. Jerome-O'Keefe (Ed.), **Global vision: Proceedings of the 37th Annual Conference of the American translators Association.** (pp. 77-89). Alexandria, VA: American Translators Association.

Miles, M., & Huberman, M. (1994). **Qualitative Data Analysis.** Thousand Oaks, CA; Sage Publications.

Morrow, P. (1994). **Legal Interpreting in Alaska. Alaska Justice Forum,** 10, 4, 24-34.

O'Barr, W. (1982). **Linguistic Evidence: Language, Power and Strategy in the Courtroom.** New York, NY: Academic Press.

O'Malley, M. & A. Chamot. (1996). **Learning strategies in second language acquisition.** Cambridge, MA: Cambridge University Press.

Patrie, C. (1989). Consecutive interpretation between English and American Sign Language. In D.L. Hammond (Ed.), **Coming of age: Proceedings of the 30th Annual Conference of the American Translators Association.** (pp. 155-162), Medford, NJ: Learned Information.

Patrie, C. (1990). Bridging the instructional gap between consecutive and simultaneous interpreting. In A.L. Willson (Ed.), **Looking ahead: Proceedings of the 31st Annual Conference of the American Translators Association.** (pp. 59-65). Medford, NJ: Learned Information.

Patrie, C. (1995). Sequencing in interpreter education. In P.W.Krawutschke (Ed.), **Connections: Proceedings of the 36th Annual Conference of the American Translators Association.** (pp. 459-470). Melford, NJ: Information Today.

Patton, M.Q. (1990). **Qualitative Evaluation and Research Methods.** Newbury Park: Sage Publications.

Pettito, L. (1993). On the otogenetic requirements for early language. In Boysson-bardies, deSchonen, Jusczykm Macneilage & Morton (Eds.), **Developmental neurocognition: speech and face processing in the first year of life.** (pp. 365-383). Washington, DC: Kluwer Academic Press.

Polit, D. & Hungler, B. (1995). **Nursing Research: Principles and Methods.** Philadelphia, PA: J. B. Lippincott Co.

Roy, C. (1992). A sociolinguistic analysis of the interpreter's role in simultaneous talk in a face-to-face interpreted dialogue. **Sign Language Studies,** 74, 21-61.

Schein, J., Mallory, B., & Greaves, S. (1991). **Communication for Deaf Students in Mainstream Classes.** Edmonton, Alberta: University of Alberta.

Seleskovitch, D. (1978). **Interpreting for international conferences.** Washington, DC: Pen and Booth.

Seleskovitch, D., & Lederer, M. (1995). **A systematic approach to teaching interpretation.** Paris, France: Didier Erudition.

Sen, A. (1994). Objectivity and position Assessment of Health, L.C. Chen, Aklienman, N. Ware eds. **Health and Social Changes.** Cambridge,MA: Harvard University Press.

Shaughnessy, J. & Zechmeister, E. (1994). **Research Methods in Psychology.** New York, NY: McGraw-Hill

Sternberg, R. (1996). **Cognitive Psychology.** Fort Worth, TX: Harcourt Brace College Publishers.

Taylor, M. (1993). **Assessment for English to ASL Interpretation.** Unpublished dissertation, University of Alberta, Edmonton, AB, Canada.

Tommol, J. & Hyona, J. (1990). **Mental load in listening, speech shadowing and simultaneous interpreting.** Paper presented at the Meeting of the World Congress of Applied Linguistics (Thessaloniki, Greece, April 15-21, 1990).

Thomsen, M. (1996). **A discourse analysis of eight spontaneous conversation narratives in American Sign Language: A case study.** Unpublished doctoral dissertation, University of California, Los Angeles.

Viaggia, S. (1991). **Teaching beginners to shut up and listen. A conference interpreter espouses silence.** Paper presented at the Annual Meeting of the First Language international Conference (Elsinore, Denmark, May 31-June 2, 1991.)

Winston, E. (1995). Spatial mapping in comparative discourse frames. In K. Emmorey & J. Reilly (Eds.), **Language, Gesture and Space.** (pp. 87-117). Hillsdale, NJ: Lawrence Erlbaum Associates.

APPENDIX

RESEARCH METHODOLOGY

Appendix

RESEARCH METHODOLOGY

The design of this study was a comparison between the accuracy of simultaneous interpreting to consecutive interpreting across three courtroom events. In this appendix the design and method of the study are presented. The description of the participants is followed by an overview of the measurement instruments, the procedure used in the collection of the data, the procedures used to analyze the results, ethical considerations, and the potential limitations of the research.

The Design

This was exploratory research based on quasi-experimental design principles as described in Campbell and Stanley (1963). Specifically, the study used a factorial design, as described in Table 6.1. The study manipulated one independent variable: the type of interpretation. The type of interpretation, consecutive or simultaneous interpreting, was studied across three conditions. These conditions included the presentation of expert witness testimony, the entering of direct evidence, and the cross-examination of the direct evidence.

Table 6.1
Factorial Design Summary

Type of Interpretation

Type of Content	Simultaneous (A1)	Consecutive (A2)
Expert Witness (B1)	A1/B1	A2/B1
Direct Evidence (B2)	A1/B2	A2/B2
Cross-Examination (B3)	A1/B3	A2/B3

The research used a blend of quantitative and qualitative approaches, which were chosen because they are both epistemologically sound and effective in obtaining the desired information to answer the research questions. The strength of a quasi-experimental design is its practicality, feasibility, and, to a certain extent, generalizability. In the real world, it is often impractical, if not impossible, to conduct true experiments. Quasi-experimental designs are research plans that introduce some controls over extraneous variables when full experimental control is lacking (Campbell and Stanley, 1963). The post-trial interviews conducted with the research participants allowed for rich, qualitative data to emerge which strengthened the research findings.

Mock Trials

The four mock trials were conducted over a two day period with the schedule as set out in Table 6.2. For each trial, a new team of lawyers, interpreters and judge was assigned. The expert witness participated in all four trials. The two Deaf witnesses each participated in one simultaneous trial and one consecutive trial. Each time the Deaf witness played the same role and participated in the same trial, but with different lawyers, judges, and interpreters.

Each separate trial involved interpreting teams, lawyers, the Deaf and non-deaf witness and the judge. The trials were conducted over a two-day period, and there were two trials per day, which replicated a typical courthouse schedule. The interpreting teams completed one trial per day in either the morning or afternoon time slot (See Table 6.2). By interpreting one trial per day, fatigue should not have been an issue hampering performance.

Table 6.2
Mock Trial Schedule

Day	Time	Type of Interpreting	Team
One	10:00 a.m. - 11:30 a.m.	Simultaneous	Team 1
	2:00 p.m. - 3:30 p.m.	Consecutive	Team 2
Two	10:00 a.m. - 11:30 a.m.	Consecutive	Team 3
	2:00 p.m. - 3:30 p.m.	Simultaneous	Team 4

The courtroom simulations consisted of 60 to 90 minute trials, involving charges of sexual assault or sexual abuse. This content area was chosen as it represented content where the possibility and consequences of interpreting errors are the gravest. Additionally, the trials included the following aspects:

1. One non-deaf expert witness gave testimony regarding deafness, American Sign Language, Deaf culture and interpretation issues. These areas were chosen to represent the discourse frame of presenting technical evidence at a consultative or formal register. During this testimony the interpreters performed English to ASL interpretation.

2. One Deaf witness gave testimony regarding sexual assault (Regina vs. Westerland) and one Deaf witness provided testimony regarding physical assault (Regina vs. Howard). The witness gave direct evidence and then was cross-examined by the defense lawyer. Entering direct evidence and the subsequent cross-examination were chosen in order to allow for two different discourse frames to emerge, that of providing one's narrative and then being challenged on that evidence.

Mock Trial Content

The courtroom interactions took place in the context of mock criminal trials. Mock trials have most of the elements present in real trials in that a judge presides, experienced lawyers perform in the trials and the court material is based on previous cases tried in Canadian courts. Participants were prepared for the mock trials in the same manner as would occur in a real trial.

The contents of each mock trial was based on simulation materials produced by the Law Courts Education Society of British Columbia. The materials have been pilot-tested for effectiveness and are used in the education of university law students and with high school students. The mock trials were developed by judges and are based on real trials that have taken place in British Columbia.

The mock trial materials were assembled in a package which included general information about the trial, plus a trial script, sample indictment sheets, the rules of examination, rules of evidence and a trial script summary. Additional sections included the description of roles and information needed for the judge, Crown counsel, and defence counsel. Where appropriate there were police file notes, and exhibits.

Out of six different trials included in the package, two criminal trials were chosen for the study. Each trial was conducted twice over the course of two days. When the trial was conducted a second time it was with different lawyers and interpreters, as well as a different judge. The mock trials were intended to be honest dramatizations of the evidence that was presented to the court during that trial. The trials were rated as advanced mock trials, suitable for participants with legal and courtroom experience. The lawyers and judges participating in this trial were all experienced practitioners which allowed for the simulation to be conducted as it would in a real court. The trials were conducted in the Moot Court at the University of Calgary's Faculty of Law building. The trials demanded that participants familiarize themselves with the deeper issues raised by the cases, by preparing for the trial and the multiplicity of issues that could arise.

Each participating lawyer and judge received a full photocopy of the mock trial material, appropriate for their role, two weeks prior to the mock trial event. The material was useful to the participants in providing an overview of the trial content and alleged offense. Lawyers were then able to prepare questions for the witnesses and review the fact sheets. Judges reviewed the cases and prepared to hear the evidence during the mock trial.

The experience level of all of the lawyers and judges allowed for the cases to proceed as if they were "real" trials; each lawyer had prepared questions to be asked of witnesses, and created new lines of questioning as the evidence was entered. Judges intervened as necessary and took responsibility to swear the witnesses and interpreters. As well, the experience level of the Deaf witnesses allowed for a natural simulation of what typically happens in a court room. The Deaf witnesses had an opportunity to meet with the Crown counsel prior to the trials, in the same manner that they would have in an actual trial, were offered sample questions and encouraged to tell their stories as honestly and clearly as possible. In addition, the Deaf witnesses had previous experience with courtroom interactions and had performed in mock or role play situations before. One of the Deaf witnesses had acted as a Deaf interpreter in many trials and was able to bring that experience to these mock trials. The expert witness had testified in over twenty trials in the same areas in which she was qualified for in the mock trials, and thus was able to bring that experience to add to the naturalness of the simulation.

Mock Trial Scenarios

Regina vs. Westerland:

The script is based on the trial of an individual who was charged with sexual assault as a result of events that occurred in Bella Coola on January 6, 1991. The Deaf witness played the part of the alleged victim. A non-deaf male witness played the role of the alleged perpetrator. He did not give evidence during the trial.

The scenario is one in which a group of friends are celebrating after a day of skiing at a ski resort. Alcohol and illegal drugs are used by some members of the group. After a period of time, the alleged victim retires to her bed. She is awakened by a male who is sexually assaulting her.

Regina vs. Howard:

This trial explores an alleged assault with a weapon, perpetrated by a teacher upon a student. The case is based on the case of Regina v. Swanson, which was tried in the B.C. Provincial Court at Massett in 1993. The Deaf witness played the part of the alleged victim. A non-deaf female played the role of the alleged perpetrator. She did not give evidence during the trial.

The scenario is one in which a young female student alleges that a teacher has assaulted her during a woodworking class, using a hammer as a weapon.

Mock Trial Procedure

Each case study proceeded as any trial does: opening remarks by judges, Crown counsel and defence counsel, the swearing of interpreters and witnesses, presentation and acceptance of expert witness, entering of expert witness testimony, calling and entering of Deaf witness testimony and cross-examination of the Deaf witness.

Each case study had a team of two interpreters assigned to the trial, and it was their responsibility to meet with the agents of the court prior to the trial, in order to review their role and describe the nature of the interpreting process. The interpreting team also had a sufficient time prior to the trial to meet the Deaf witness and to familiarize themselves with the witness's language use and background.

During the trials, there were no other witnesses or observers present in the body of the court.

Recruitment of Participants

Investigation into the feasibility of research began approximately twelve months prior to the study. It was important to determine if (a) interpreters would want to have their work examined for accuracy, (b) under what conditions, (c) which mock trial materials would be most suitable, and (d) what agents of the court (lawyers and judges) would be willing to participate. It was determined that eight lawyers, four judges, and four interpreters were needed for the study.

Approval was sought and gained from several organizations in order to conduct the study. Ethics approval was first gained from the Department of Education Psychology Ethical Review Committee and the Faculty of Education Joint Research Ethics Committee (University of Calgary). Then the Law Courts Education Society of British Columbia gave approval to purchase and use any of six criminal mock trials that were developed by Judge C. Cunliffe Barnett. Lawyers and Judges in the Calgary area were approached and consented to be involved with this project. Deaf witnesses from Alberta and British Columbia were contacted and consented to be involved in the study.

An expert witness from British Columbia was approached and gave consent to participate. Finally, the Faculty of Law, University of Calgary, was approached and their cooperation was instrumental in securing the Moot Court within the Faculty of Law Building.

A purposeful sampling technique was used in this study for the selection of participants. According to Patton (1990), qualitative research typically provides an in-depth focus on a small purposefully selected sample. The logic and power of purposeful sampling lies in its ability to offer information-rich cases for in-depth study. Criterion sampling is one type of purposeful sampling. Several criteria were chosen for selection of participants in this study. In order to obtain data from participants who knew best about the process of interpreting, interpreters with significant years of experience in interpreting were chosen. Additionally, lawyers were selected on the basis of criminal law training and experience, and a suitable number of years of experience at the bar. Lawyers who did not have experience in criminal law or who had little courtroom experience were not invited to participate. Interpreters who did not perform interpreting in legal settings were also not invited to participate.

The interpreter participants were all non-deaf and three were certified from the national accrediting body, the Association of Visual Language Interpreters of Canada. Two interpreters held previous certification with the American certifying body, the Registry of Interpreters for the Deaf.

Three female interpreters and one male interpreter were chosen. They were selected from the communities of Toronto, Ontario; Winnipeg, Manitoba; Edmonton, Alberta and Vancouver, British Columbia. All are fluent users of American Sign Language and English, and have extensive interpreting experience. All are respected members of their communities, and active in their professional associations, community-based organizations of the Deaf and attend professional development opportunities regularly.

The following selection criteria were applied to the participants.

Lawyers

Lawyers participating in this study were limited to those who had practiced criminal law for a minimum of three years, and had at least 150 hours of actual courtroom experience. The lawyers were recruited from Alberta, through contact with the Faculty of Law, University of Calgary and via professional contacts among the legal community in Calgary.

Expert Witness

Non-deaf expert witnesses participating in this study were limited to those individuals who had prior experience testifying as expert witnesses in matters of sexual abuse or sexual assault, or language and interpretation issues. These witnesses were recruited through recommendations made by the University of Calgary, Faculty of Law, Dean's Office and via the researcher's own professional contacts.

Deaf Witnesses

Deaf witnesses participating in this study were limited to those individuals who attended a school for the deaf, used American Sign Language as their preferred language, regularly socialized within the Deaf community, and had experience using professional interpreters. While the goal was to recruit equal numbers of female and male witnesses, the study proceeded with two female Deaf witnesses. Deaf community members were recruited from the communities of Calgary, Edmonton, and Vancouver, through contact with local Deaf associations. Additional contact was made with the Vancouver chapter of Women Against Violence Against Women, in an attempt to recruit female Deaf witnesses who previously had participated in a series of video productions focused on sexual assault education and prevention, and hence had an established comfort range for participating in the proposed simulation. This attempt was not successful.

Interpreters

Four professional ASL/English interpreters served as the subjects of this study. They were selected from interpreting communities in the cities of Toronto, Edmonton, Winnipeg and Vancouver. Participation in the study was limited to those interpreters who were nationally certified by the Canadian professional body, the Association of Visual Language Interpreters of Canada (AVLIC), had a minimum of five years interpreting experience in legal settings, and had a minimum of 150 hours of courtroom experience. One interpreter who is not yet certified was chosen, based on the person's extensive experience in interpreting in legal settings (see Table 6.3). Additionally, interpreters were chosen for their experience in using both simultaneous and consecutive forms of interpretation in legal settings. Interpreters were recruited via written notices posted in the national newsletter of the professional interpreting association and via personal contacts made with interpreters.

Table 6.3
Overview of Interpreter Participants

Interpreter	Gender	Certification	Years Signing	Legal Experience
A	Male	none	15	1000 hours
B	Female	COI	35	3000 hours
C	Female	COI	40	150 hours
D	Female	COI	22	2000 hours

Note: COI is the acronym for Certificate of Interpretation, the national ASL/English certification offered in Canada.

Descriptive Characteristics of Participants

Lawyers/Judge Participants

Nine lawyers and three judges participated in this study. All were from Calgary, Alberta. Four of the nine lawyers had previous experience working with spoken language interpreters (Croatian, Vietnamese, Cree, and French) and two lawyers had previous experience working with sign language interpreters. These lawyers indicated they had witnessed simultaneous and consecutive interpretation over the span of their practice. In addition, three of the lawyers had participated in a law school orientation which addressed some issues of deafness and interpretation given by a Calgary based organization. The remaining five lawyers had no personal experience working with interpreters and had not met a Deaf person prior to participating in the study.

One of the judges had extensive experience working with interpreters (aboriginal languages) and had experienced consecutive interpretation in several trials. A second judge had never seen a sign language interpreter working in the courtroom and while he had some experience with spoken language interpreters, he described his exposure as "limited" (see Tables 6.4 and 6.5). The third judge had experience with both spoken and sign language interpreters.

Table 6.4
Overview of Lawyer and Judge Participants

Gender	Occupation	Years of Legal Experience
Male	Judge	36
Male	Judge	23
Male	Judge	24
Female	Lawyer	10
Male	Lawyer	15
Male	Lawyer	24
Male	Lawyer	30
Male	Lawyer	4
Male	Lawyer	25
Male	Lawyer	4
Male	Lawyer	4
Male	Lawyer	5

Table 6.5   **Detailed Overview of Experience of
                        Lawyers and Judges**

Role	Gender	Legal Experience
Judge A	Male	Practiced criminal law 15 years; Provincial Court judge for 29 years; no experience with ASL interpreters; currently Family & Youth Court Bench
Judge B	Male	Practiced criminal law 20 years; Provincial Court judge - Criminal Courts Division for 3 years; experience with spoken language interpreters
Judge C	Male	Senior Crown prosecutor; extensive experience with interpreters; acted as judge in this study
Lawyer A	Male	Private criminal practice, admitted to bar 5 years ago; no experience with interpreters
Lawyer B	Female	Private criminal practice, admitted to bar 10 years ago; no experience with interpreters
Lawyer C	Male	Private criminal practice, admitted to bar 15 years ago; no experience with interpreters
Lawyer D	Male	Private criminal practice, admitted to bar 24 years ago; limited experience with spoken language interpreters

Table 6.5 (cont.)		Detailed Overview of Experience of Lawyers and Judges
Role	**Gender**	**Legal Experience**
Lawyer E	Male	Queen's Counsel; Private criminal practice, admitted to bar 30 years ago; extensive experience with sign & spoken language interpreters
Lawyer F	Male	Private criminal practice, admitted to bar 25 years ago; no experience with interpreters
Lawyer G	Male	Private criminal practice, admitted to bar 4 years ago; law school orientation to deafness and interpreters
Lawyer H/ Judge D	Male	Acted as judge in this study; Private criminal practice, admitted to bar 5 years ago; limited experience with spoken language interpreters
Lawyer I	Male	Private criminal practice, admitted to bar 4 years ago; law school orientation to deafness and interpreters
Lawyer J	Male	Private criminal practice, admitted to bar 4 years ago.

Deaf Witnesses

Two female Deaf participants were selected to perform in the role of the witnesses. Both are members of the Deaf community, and are fluent users of American Sign Language. They socialize in their respective local Deaf communities and work as ASL instructors and program coordinators. Both have taught in interpreter education programs, teaching ASL and Deaf culture.

One Deaf participant is also an interpreter, functioning as a Deaf interpreter in legal and court matters. She has completed a two-year interpreter education program and has extensive experience working with non-deaf ASL/English interpreters. At the time the study was conducted she was in her mid-forties and had used ASL since she was four years of age. She attended a provincial school for the deaf for much of her early education, and then attended college, accessing the post-secondary studies though the provision of interpreting services.

The second Deaf participant has a degree from an American university in Sign Language Studies and continues to teach and coordinate sign language programs. At the time the study was conducted she was in her early thirties and had used ASL since she was five years of age. She attended a program for deaf students for much of her early education, and then attended Gallaudet University in Washington, D.C. Her education was provided in American Sign Language by professors who could sign and by using interpreters.

Expert Witness

The expert witness was a female who has over 35 years of experience working in the Deaf community. She holds a doctorate, and coordinates an interpreter education program. She has been an expert witness in over 30 trials and is frequently called upon to organize and supervise teams of interpreters working in legal contexts. Her expert testimony was specific to the areas of American Sign Language, Deaf culture, and matters of interpretation. She holds certification as an interpreter from AVLIC and RID, and is viewed as a master interpreter by her peers. Her international reputation as an author, presenter and interpreter-educator is well established.

Procedures for Data Collection

Four different types of data were collected in this research:

1. Preparation conversations were audiotaped between interpreters, between interpreters and witnesses, and between interpreters and lawyers;
2. Videotaped simultaneous and consecutive interpretation gathered from the four trials, across three discourse frames;
3. Interpreting notes taken and used by the interpreters during each trial; and
4. Interviews with all participants after the trial experiences.

Preparation of Participants for the Mock Trials

It was important for Deaf witnesses to be prepared for the trial experience, just as they would be if they were participating in a real criminal trial. This preparation occurred approximately 10 to 14 days prior to the event, and on the day of the trial. Preparation was conducted by a Deaf person who has had considerable experience with courtroom interactions, and a non-deaf expert witness who had extensive experience with courtroom interactions involving Deaf people. These two people prepared the witnesses so that they could understand the nature of the experience, and to predict possible questions and responses within the simulation.

The interpreters participating in the research also engaged in preparation exercises, similar to those in accepting a real court appointment. They were advised of the criminal charges, the names of the participants and the purpose of the interaction. Additionally, interpreters were offered notetaking guidelines, as a tool for providing consecutive interpreting. They could choose to use the technique or not based on their personal preferences for managing the interpreting process. Any notes taken during the trials were collected after the trial for analysis.

The conversations held between the assigned team of interpreters while preparing for the event were videotaped and/or audiotaped, as were the preparation conversations held between interpreters and lawyers.

The lawyers and judges received a briefing

sheet describing the interpreting processes, along with the materials from the British Columbia Legal Education Society describing the nature of the trial. They were oriented to the experience of working with interpreters by the interpreting team working each trial. During this same preparation interview, lawyers had the option to prepare the interpreters for the line of questioning and evidence to be brought forward.

Recording the Courtroom Discourse

One of the difficulties in collecting data from real-life interpreted court events involves technological and procedural challenges. The necessary use of video technology in recording ASL data has long been faced by sign language linguists. Use of recording devices in interpreted events can be especially problematic. For example, in order to interpret between ASL and English, interpreters must be positioned so that they can both see and be seen by the Deaf consumer. Yet, analysis requires that both the Deaf participants' and the interpreters' signing be visibly accessible in the camera view.

The mock trials were conducted in the Moot Court at the University of Calgary's Law Faculties Building. The Moot Court is permanently equipped to videotape participants and the equipment is built into the design of the courtroom, meaning there is a relatively unmarked presence of multiple cameras in the courtroom environment. This advanced technology offers the advantage of making all parties visible on the videotapes, and can be used to obtain data that offer access and insights potentially unavailable in an actual interpreted encounter. Each videotape had time codes inserted into them, aiding transcription processes.

For the purposes of recording pre-courtroom conversations between interpreters, and interpreters and lawyers, an audiotape recording device was used.

Interviews

In-depth interviews were also chosen as a way of securing detailed information about the participants' perceptions of the experience. Lasslett and Rapport (cited in Mishler, 1986) note that interviews offer the advantage of greater depth, and require greater interaction between researcher and participants. The success of the interview is dependent on: (1) open communication to establish trust and rapport between the parties; (2) the researcher's personal involvement to facilitate the process; and, (3) the interviewer's skills in discourse analysis (Brenner, 1985; Gluck, 1979).

There are three types of interviews identified in the literature: the structured interview, the semi-structured interview , and the unstructured interview (Berg, 1995; Mishler, 1986; Kirby and McKenna, 1996). Feminist interviewing practices that emphasize semi-structured and unstructured interview techniques maximize discovery and description through the ideas, thoughts, and memories in the person's words (Reinharz, 1992).

This study employed semi-structured and unstructured interviewing approaches. The interviews were conducted following the courtroom data collection. Interviews were conducted with all four interpreters, as well as with the Deaf and non-deaf witnesses, the lawyers, and the judge in each trial. The purpose of the interviews was to clarify the recorded data and to develop a deeper appreciation of being reliant on the interpretation (Deaf and non-deaf consumers, lawyers, judges).

The interviews with Deaf participants were conducted in American Sign Language, and the interviews with all non-deaf participants were conducted in spoken English. Transcription of English interviews was based on the audiotaped recording of the interviews, and the transcription of the interviews conducted in ASL was based on notes taken by the researcher during the interview.

The interview questions were open-ended in order to have more flexibility in probing. This approach served to keep the interview focused while allowing individual perspectives and expectations to emerge. All interviews with the interpreters were conducted in a meeting room in the Faculty of Law Building at the University of Calgary. All interviews with lawyers and judges were held in their offices. The interviews were conducted individually so that the participants would have the maximum freedom to air their views. Informal conversational interviews happened in a large meeting room during the course of the two day experiment, during breaks and at the conclusion of the taping of the trials.

At the beginning of each interview I expressed the purpose of the interview - to conduct research for my doctoral dissertation - and my gratitude for the respondent's participation in the study and the interview. This helped to establish rapport with interviewees and also helped to maintain a perceived neutral identity. In this study, a total of 19 data collection interviews were conducted after the mock trial events.

Data Analysis

Criteria for Videotaped Data Analysis

In interpretation research, the fundamental step of generating data from observations is made by assessing the degree to which the response protocols match or mismatch the input text (Dillinger, 1994). This is done by categorizing the propositional information units of the original text as "absent", "recalled", "inferred", or "recalled with inference" in the response protocol (Dillinger, 1994). This approach was adopted for this study. In propositional analysis, propositions serve as the units of meaning, representing the "structural meaning" of an utterance, and an utterance is made up of a head concept (predicator), a list of concepts (fillers), and their relations (slots) to the head concept (Dillinger, 1994). An example may serve to illustrate this approach:

> Utterance: "John assaulted you two times this month?"
>
> HEAD: assaulted (specific reference needed in ASL)
>
> AGENT: John
>
> OBJECT: you (specific pronoun needed in ASL)

As Dillinger (1994) describes, the slots (capital letters) are semantic relations derived from the work of Fillmore (1968) and Gruber (1976). This type of analysis is standard practice for representing utterance meanings, and serves as one part of the analysis strategy.

For the purpose of this initial analysis, each **proposition** received a score according to the degree of similarity between it and the segment of the interpretation being analyzed, using the following scale of similarity:

0 - the slot-filler pair is not present in the segment.

1 - there is a change of meaning in either the slot or the filler (semantic change).

2 - there is a change in the surface form of the either the slot or the filler, without a change in meaning (paraphrase).

3 - the slot-filler pair appeared in the segment

verbatim (verbatim).

4 - the slot-filler pair appeared in the segment in its equivalent language form.

This coding approach has been used with broad applicability across languages (Dillinger, 1994). The semantic relations appear as language universals and have been used in the analysis of a wide variety of languages. This type of linguistic analysis does have its limitations, however, in terms of not capturing the affectual components of an utterance, nor does it allow for an analysis of discourse frames, and main point/supporting point detail equivalency.

In order to address these limitations, a further detailed analysis of utterances was applied, using discourse frames, affect, and main point/supporting point(s) detail levels. The musical score transcription system allowed for an utterance by utterance conveyance of these properties, which yielded a more complete analysis of the data. Again, an ordering system was applied to each of the levels of analysis. For example, **discourse frames** were analyzed as:

0 - speaker/signer goal is absent in the utterance.

1 - speaker/signer goal is changed in the utterance.

2 - speaker/signer goal is accurately analyzed and presented within the utterance.

3 - speaker/signer goal is accurately analyzed
and presented within the utterance, and has
the desired impact/contextual force upon the
receiver.

Similarly, affect, and main points and supporting detail were analyzed and an ordinal system
applied to each level of analysis. **Affect** was examined for the following levels:

0 - affect of speaker/signer is lost in the
interpreted utterance.

1 - affect of the speaker/signer is changed in the
interpreted utterance.

2 - affect of the speaker/signer is accurately
conveyed within the utterance.

3 - affect of the speaker/signer is accurately
conveyed within the utterance and has the
desired impact/contextual force upon the
receiver.

Main point (similar to Dillinger's use of
"Head" concept) **and supporting detail** was analyzed and the following system applied to it:

0 - main point(s) and supporting detail is lost
in the interpreted utterance.

1 - main point is changed and supporting
detail is changed in the interpreted
utterance.

2 - main point(s) and supporting detail(s) are analyzed accurately and conveyed in the interpreted utterance.

3 - main point(s) and the supporting detail(s) are analyzed accurately and conveyed in the interpreted utterance, and has the desired impact/contextual force upon the receiver.

All data was reviewed by the researcher with assistance from both native signers and qualified interpreters (both hearing and Deaf) to promote accuracy. Validity checks were performed by additional research team members, and included native signers and qualified interpreters, who are both certified and have extensive experience in legal interpretation.

Video Data Transcription

The transcription of discourse in any language involves consideration of a variety of theoretical issues (Metzger, 1995). However, the problems facing sign language transcription are even greater than those faced by spoken language linguists, as a result of the unwritten status of signed languages and their articulatory complexities. Winston (1994) offers advice to researchers, suggesting the need to include visual and spatial information, and the need for consistency in the use of transcription symbols. ASL does not have a written form, and because of the nature of the language, there exist multiple articulators (including fingers, hands, arms, shoulders, neck, head, mouth, cheeks, eyes and eyebrows), hence written transcription can lose more of the original than it captures (Metzger, 1995).

A transcription reflects and emphasizes what the transcriber thinks is relevant within the data. For this reason Ochs (1979) and Metzger (1995) suggest that transcripts should be based on theoretical goals. The focus of the current study is to analyze the interpreters' utterances as they interact with the courtroom discourse as a whole, hence a musical score format of transcription was adopted.

Metzger (1995) suggests a musical score format of transcription is one way of representing the simultaneous and overlapping nature of interactive discourse and allows for the indication of discourse phenomena such as pausing. Such a format allows the sequence of events to unfold from left to right on a horizontal line, while the list of participants occurring from top-to-bottom allows each person's utterances to be captured within a single moment of overlap.

The musical score format has been used successfully by ASL researchers and found to be particularly useful when recording and analyzing interpreted encounters. As Metzger (1995) identifies, most of what is uttered by non-interpreter participants (i.e. lawyers, witnesses, judge) is re-uttered by the interpreter. In simultaneous interpretation, this leads to a tremendous amount of overlap throughout the data. Moreover, because the interpreter not only uses two languages but two modalities as well, it is possible that she will produce utterances in more that one modality at one a time (both signing and speaking). In order to accurately and unambiguously represent the interpreter's utterances, two lines of transcription are ascribed to the interpreter throughout the data analyzed: one for English utterances and the other for ASL utterances.

Certain transcription conventions related to both spoken and signed language transcription were adhered to within the transcript. For example, the transcription incorporates both etic (focus on the form of the sign) and emic (focus on the meaning of given sign) description of signs. As well, nonmanual and contextual information is included where necessary to enhance readability of the transcript.

Translations of the ASL are provided where necessary to make the transcript more accessible. The transcript was prepared by the researcher, with assistance from both native signers and qualified interpreters (both hearing and Deaf) to promote accuracy.

Every attempt has been made in the current study to address these theoretical issues, especially as they relate to multiparty, bilingual, interpreted discourse.

Data Analysis of Written Materials

Analysis of Preparation Work by Interpreters

The conversations of interpreters working in teams to prepare for the trials were conducted in spoken English, and were audiotaped for later transcription by professional transcribers. All preparation data was examined for patterns and themes, and context charts and event-state network charts serve to illustrate the data. A context chart is a network, mapping in graphic form the interrelationships among the roles and groups that make up the context of the behaviour. An event-state network chart helped to identify those series of events relevant to the preparation stage (Miles and Huberman, 1994).

Analysis of Notes Used by Interpreters during Trials

The notes taken and used by interpreters in the trials were analyzed. If miscues were present in either the notes or trial interpretation, the notes were reviewed for miscue analysis. For example, the notes may have showed the source message was comprehended accurately by the interpreter, but that the target language composition was inaccurate. Cokely's Sociolinguistic Model (1993) served as a guide for identifying the stage(s) of the interpreting process which resulted in miscues. The final stage of data analysis and data classification for the notes was content analysis which involved identifying coherent and important examples, themes, and patterns in the data.

Analysis of Interviews

Interviews were analyzed using identical methods as described above. That is, interviews conducted in spoken English were transcribed by professional transcribers. Interviews conducted in ASL were not interpreted into spoken English, but rather the researcher's notes were transcribed by professional transcribers.

Data was organized immediately after data collection. First, the raw data were checked to ensure they were complete and sorted out per categories - interpreters, lawyers and judges, and witnesses. All interview data were examined for patterns and themes, and context charts served to illustrate the data. The next step was to classify the data, for which a classification system was crucial. Natural variations in the data were noted, and categories emerged, such as, attitudes towards interpretation provided in consecutive mode versus simultaneous mode, the impact of interpreting decisions on lawyer's questioning techniques, the impact of interpreting decisions on a Deaf witness's participation in the court interaction, and the need for accurate interpretation in order to form impressions about witnesses. These categories contributed to a greater understanding of the participants' attitudes and experiences of working with interpreters in the courtroom setting.

Ethical Considerations

A major ethical issue in this study was to avoid identifying the interpreter participants. Interpreters form a small group of professionals in Canada and those who work in legal settings are an even smaller subset of the interpreter population. For segments of data to be shown in professional venues, written permission was secured from each of the interpreter participants.

The study explored interpretation accuracy within a given context, that is, courtroom interactions. The findings are not intended to be generalized to suggest that the practices of these participants represent all interpreters in Canada. Instead, this study has explored how a group of participants - interpreters, Deaf and non-deaf witnesses, lawyers and judges view the issues surrounding accurate courtroom interpretation. The findings of this research do however make a connection between this specific legal context and the broader issues affecting interpretation practice and interpreter pedagogy.

Komesaroff (1998) states: "To expose personal influences that may affect the interpretation of data is not only legitimate for researchers, but their responsibility" (p. 80). Similarly, I have attempted to disclose my support for both simultaneous and consecutive interpretation, and accurate bilingual-bicultural interpretation processes. This does not appear to have been an obstacle to discussing or investigating the ideas that were key to this research or to the fairness of the analysis and reporting of data.

Measures to Enhance Trustworthiness of the Study

Lincoln and Guba (1985) suggest that it is important to establish trustworthiness as distinguished from validity and reliability. They suggest that credibility, transferability, dependability and confirmability are the criteria for trustworthiness and outline several strategies to achieve these qualities. Kirk and Miller (1986) identify that there are no perfect methods for collecting and analyzing data, but using more than one data collection method and one data source, spending adequate time in the field, persistence in gathering trustworthy data, and clear and detailed documentation of fieldnotes are all effective ways to obtain trustworthy data and to develop meaningful interpretations.

The concept of triangulation is also useful in enhancing credibility, validity and reliability in qualitative research (Patton, 1990). There are four methods of triangulation: methods triangulation, triangulation of sources, analyst triangulation and theory/perspective triangulation.

Several approaches were used to enhance the trustworthiness of this research. The purposeful sampling technique ensured information-rich data. The participants had significant professional experience in interpreting, and the lawyers were extremely competent criminal trial lawyers. The judges had lengthy trial experience to supplement their judicial experience. All participants were able to provide rich and relevant information. As well, the data sources included interpreters, lawyers, judges, and witnesses, thus expanding the information on the research problem. The sources complemented and supplemented each other. Two peer analysts reviewed the coded materials and commented on them. Two other linguistic experts were invited to verify samples of interpretation chosen to be included in the dissertation. As well, there were well-organized systematic records and the video-taped case studies could be referred to conveniently. Finally, the research process was well documented. All methods, procedures and considerations were described in detail. These measures serve to illustrate how the findings were generated and analyzed, and thus add to the trustworthiness of study conclusions.

Factors Jeopardizing Internal and External Validity

Campbell and Stanley (1963) present several classes of extraneous variables that must be considered and controlled in the research design. These variables, if not controlled, might produce effects confounded with the effect of the experimental stimulus. In this study, the research design attempted to

control for the elements of testing, experiment conditions, maturation, instrumentation, selection of
subjects, and contamination. The following summarizes how each of the threats to validity was
addressed in this study.

Testing
          The effects of taking a test upon the scores
of a second testing has relevance to this research, in
that the interpreters provided interpretation in one
trial, and then a second trial. By interpreting a second trial, they could have performed better than the
first trial. This effect was addressed by counter-bal-
ancing the interpreters on each team, and by sepa-
rating the type of interpretation per trial. The interpreters did not provide interpretation of the same
type over the two trials, and the content of the two
trials differed.

Conditions
          The threat to validity to be addressed here
was the need for consistency among the conditions.
When conditions vary, the researcher has allowed
for rival explanations to creep into the study. In this
study, a number of conditions were held constant or
balanced. For example, each trial utilized the same
degree of preparation material which was made
available to the interpreters and lawyers. As well,
the length and complexity of the trials were identical. Each trial involved the same number of witnesses: one Deaf witness and one expert witness
giving testimony. Each Deaf witness was assigned

to one trial in which consecutive interpreting was used and one trial in which simultaneous interpreting was used. The expert witness remained constant throughout the four trials. Interpreters were allowed to prepare for the work with each other, as well as consult with the lawyers and witnesses prior to the trials. The process of consultation was identical for each trial.

Maturation Effects

The threat to internal validity to be addressed was that of processes within the participants operating as a function of the passage of time per se, including gaining experience, growing more tired, and so on. The study was conducted over a two day period, which ensured that the interpreters' skills and strategies were tested within a relatively short period of time, thus reducing the factor of greater experience on the quality of their work. As well, the trials were completed in a 90 minute period by two interpreters, which was consistent with the interpreters real working conditions, so fatigue was not expected to be an issue.

Instrumentation

The threat to validity in this area stems from the type of instrumentation used and potential changes in the instrument, or changes in the observers which could produce changes in the obtained measurements. In this study, the same framework for assessing the accuracy of interpretation was used consistently over the four mock trials.

As well, the framework was one that had been used in previous studies and was deemed appropriate for this investigation (Dillinger, 1994). Researcher observations and findings were reviewed by two other experts in interpretation to ensure that the instruments were applied consistently and that the findings were valid.

Selection of Interpreters

Every attempt was made in this study to balance interpreter characteristics in terms of linguistic knowledge, interpretation skill, experience in legal settings, and interpreter qualifications such as national certification. One consideration in this context is that one of the interpreter participants did not possess certification at the time of the study, however s/he had equivalent experience in legal interpreting and was viewed as having equivalent skills to a certified interpreter, despite not having taken the certification exam. The interpreters were assigned to teams and each team performed one simultaneous trial and one consecutive trial, but it is the lack of randomization in the selection of the subjects that defines this design as quasi-experimental.

Contamination

This type of threat to internal validity occurs when there is communication of information about the experiment between groups of participants. At the beginning of this study, interpreter participants were advised that they would be assigned to two trials, one each within the modes of simultaneous and consecutive interpretation. Given that both modes of interpretation were common to all subjects and that the goal was the same for each case event, that is, the most accurate interpretation the interpreters could provide, the effects of contamination may have been reduced.

It is possible that the Hawthorne effect may be inextricably linked to the area of study in that the interpreters likely wanted to perform their best work due to their awareness of the fact that the researcher was interested in the interpretation. The researcher was not present in the courtroom to observe the interpreters while the trials were being conducted, thus reducing the possible influence of the researcher's presence on the interpreters.

Generalizability

In any study it is important to consider whether the pattern of results is restricted to a particular group of subjects, setting or time. In this study, the interpreters who participated work in a variety of settings, not just courtrooms, so it is likely that the quality of interpretation provided and the kinds of errors made in this study are consistent with their interpreting work in the broader community. The three certified interpreters and one non-certified interpreter were from four different communities, yet their professional profiles were very similar. However, the nature of the research was to explore and enhance our knowledge about interpreting accuracy, in order to inform our practice. One experiment is very unlikely to answer all questions about an experimental hypothesis, and this experiment makes no claims to do that.

In this study the researcher exerted a high degree of control in the arrangement of the experimental conditions. For example, the researcher selected two different mock trials that involved criminal charges relating to sexual assault and assault. A purposeful sample using criterion sampling techniques was chosen, so that the participants represented professional sign language interpreters who were experienced in legal and courtroom interpreting. Similarly, judges and lawyers were selected from a specific community, representing criminal trial lawyers and judges in Southern Alberta.

The qualitative aspects of the study included one-to-one interviews with the participants in the study. The research used three approaches to interviewing: (1) formal interviews with an interview guide; (2) informal conversational interviews; and (3) a combination of the two (interview guide followed by an informal conversation). The interview questions were designed to focus on the experiences of the participants in the mock trials. The questions were open-ended in order to have more flexibility in probing. These approaches served to keep the interview focused while allowing individual perspectives and experiences to emerge.

All formal interviews were conducted in either a seminar room at the University of Calgary Faculty of Law building or in the offices of the participating lawyers and judges. All formal interviews with interpreters, lawyers, judges, and Deaf participants were conducted individually so that the participants might have the maximum freedom to air their views.

Informal conversational interviews occurred in University of Calgary Faculty of Law building during the breaks between mock trials.

In general, the interview guide was followed in asking the questions, but both the research participants and the researcher were not restricted to it. Some participants departed from the questions raised and offered further information that was relevant to the research. The questions were effective in triggering thoughts from the participants and required occasional follow-up questions from the researcher. Paraphrasing and summarization were also used to help the participants consolidate their views and guide the discussion.

Interviews conducted in spoken English were audiotaped with a small cassette recorder, with the participant's prior consent. No other observer or co-interviewer was present. At each interview, the researcher explained the purpose of the research and then followed the interview guide to start the discussion. As the interviews were conducted after the mock trials, a rapport was already established between the researcher and the participants, which allowed for a relaxed atmosphere to emerge.

Conclusion

The methodology used in the study was constructed to describe, in as much detail as possible, the similarities and differences in the accuracy of courtroom interpretation when the provision of interpreting services is simultaneous and consecutive. This chapter has reviewed the research methodology decisions and design principles that shaped this study. The research offered an opportunity to examine some of the key issues related to interpretation practice in a legal context, where the consequences of errors are grave.